YOU CAN'T
TAKE IT
WITH YOU

YOU CAN'T TAKE IT WITH YOU

The Common-Sense Guide to Estate Planning for Canadians

Sandra E. Foster

JOHN WILEY & SONS

Toronto • New York • Chichester • Brisbane • Singapore

John Wiley & Sons Canada Limited
22 Worcester Road
Etobicoke, Ontario
M9W 1L1

Canadian Cataloguing in Publication Data
Foster, Sandra,
    You can't take it with you: the common-sense guide to estate planning for Canadians

Includes index.
ISBN 0-471-64171-5

1. Estate planning — Canada — Popular works.
I. Title
KE5974.Z82F67 1996   346.7105'2   C96-930751-9
KF750.F67 1996

Production Credits
Cover & text design: Christine Rae
Printer: Trigraphic Printing Ltd.

Printed in Canada
10 9 8 7 6 5 4 3 2

CONTENTS

PREFACE

The stories of what happens to families on the death of a family member vary from horrendous to "everything was taken care of." Estate planning and death are difficult subjects for many Canadians to discuss, let alone plan for. It seems to be part of our Western society to deny that death will happen to us, or even to someone close to us. It is almost as if we believe that talking about death will make it happen sooner.

Many people think of a will when they think of estate planning, but it is much more. Planning your estate also involves powers of attorney, minimizing taxes and fees, health care considerations, the implications of family law, and other important issues. While estate planning can be difficult to define, it involves caring for the people around you, your community, and the assets and property that you have saved and managed.

A well-designed estate plan is one of the keys of a successful financial plan, but it is all too often overlooked. It saddens me to hear people say, "I wish we'd known about that sooner." Everyone—male, female, married, widowed, divorced, or single—regardless of their net worth, needs to consider the estate side of their financial plan. Even Canadians who do not consider themselves wealthy by traditional standards have accumulated significant estates during their lifetimes: homes, cottages, RRSPs, pension plans, jewellery, and investments. Their success has come through hard work assisted by inflation.

While doing nothing is one of your options, you will see this is not in the best interests of your family, business, or other relationships. As our society becomes more and more litigious and regulated and that estate planning is something everyone should consider. I believe that we need to take steps to keep government out of our lives wherever we can. Through estate planning, we can speak for ourselves and our families.

There are many books on the shelves that deal with financial planning or creating wealth. Most of them include only a few pages about estate planning. But at my seminars it became apparent to me that there were many questions that needed to be answered. This book is the first of its kind in Canada—a comprehensive, practical guide to estate planning for Canadians—full of examples, quotes, and questions that I have been asked. The information in this book has been developed from real-life experiences, interviews with ordinary Canadians and other professionals, the interpretation of Revenue Canada bulletins, and the applicable federal and provincial legislation. It has evolved from my research over many years.

This book is designed to help you

• assess your estate planning needs

• ask your advisors informed questions

• organize your financial affairs, and

• take the appropriate steps to implement your estate plan.

Estate planning can be straightforward or complex. There is no one perfect solution. How then do you develop and implement an estate plan to meet your own needs while you are alive as well as to benefit your beneficiaries the way that you envision? How do you balance the financial issues with your family's personal political issues? Any strategy needs to consider these differences. For example, you may want to name your adult child as the beneficiary of your RRSP. But there are certain tax advantages if you name your spouse that are not available to your children.

We will look at ways to distribute your estate, what happens on death, and the issues to be considered when assets are left to a spouse (same-generation planning), to children or grand-children (inter-generation planning), or to charity. We will discuss estate planning basics, the more commonly considered estate planning strategies and how they work, and some of the more advanced strategies, such as trust arrangements and estate freezes. We will also look at the human side of estate planning and dealing with relationships.

We will discuss some of the estate planning strategies used by others in varied situations. But the strategies discussed here should not be construed as necessarily appropriate for your own similar situation. A particular strategy or technique, considered in isolation, may appear to make sense for you until it is combined with other objectives or considerations. And then it may be completely inappropriate.

This book contains a series of checklists, quizzes, and forms for you to complete. Self-assessment is an important phase in financial planning. Besides that, by working through this information, you may be able to save some professional fees when developing your estate plan.

After reading this book and completing the quizzes and forms, you should feel more comfortable and better prepared when talking to a professional about your estate planning. Being informed will help you to determine the most effective estate plan to implement—and ensure that you do not send Revenue Canada any more than is necessary, or sooner than necessary.

 The cost of using professionals to set up your estate plan in place may be relatively small when you compare it with the hundreds or thousands of dollars saved by having a properly documented estate plan.

In the examples I use in the book, I have made the numbers as simple as possible to help you better understand the discussion. I have rounded numbers to the nearest dollar and used a 3% inflation rate and a 50% marginal tax rate, except where noted. A 50% marginal tax rate assumes that for every dollar of income, 50 cents goes to the government. But when you are assessing your own situation, use *your* numbers.

WORDS OF CAUTION

Family law and the laws related to wills, powers of attorney, trusts, living wills, and probate fees vary from province to province. This book looks at the estate planning issues for the residents of the common law provinces and comments on some of the considerations unique to particular provinces. It does not discuss estate planning issues specific to farm properties. Quebec is a civil law province—and could be the subject of another book.

This book is *not* intended to be a formal estate planning guide. (If you are a estate planning professional, please understand that the purpose of this book is to provide a foundation of estate planning information for Canadians who do not have your technical expertise.) This book is not a legal document or a tax guide. It does not provide legal advice.

Same-sex partners are not recognized by legislation covering estate planning but the amendment to the *Human Rights Act* may mean changes in the future. Use of the word "spouse" in this book does not apply to same-sex couples. It is important for people in same-sex relationships to clearly document their intentions.

This book discusses general issues and strategies to consider in preparing an estate plan. It does not exhaust all the considerations or provide solutions for every situation. It provides information of a general nature to help you understand the language of estate planning and the more common estate planning strategies. It is sold with the understanding that the information that follows is not a substitute for consulting with a professional who can apply the most current tax, trust, estate, succession, and family laws of your province to your personal situation. It is not designed so that you can "do it yourself."

The analysis in this book represents the opinion of the author and the legislation that was in effect at the time of publication. Care has been taken to ensure the accuracy of the information contained in this publication at the time it was written.

Readers are encouraged to obtain professional legal, tax, and financial advice on before deciding on a course of action.

ACKNOWLEDGEMENTS

This book reflects the knowledge and insights that I gained from research and dozens of discussions on estate planning with other professionals. I wish to acknowledge all the dedicated professionals who went before me and those who are focusing today on providing leadership in their profession and the best advice to their clients.

Special thanks to Karen Milner for her belief in this project.

Thank you to David Boyd-Thomas, Richard Chuback, lawyer, John Kane, John Mott, chartered accountant, Elaine Pantel, certified general accountant, Marilynne Seguin at Dying with Dignity, and Pat Sherbin at M.O.R.E. for reviewing the manuscript and providing many useful suggestions.

I would also like to acknowledge my husband Dave, for his unfaltering faith and support, and my children for their patience.

ESTATE PLANNING CHECKLIST

The first step in developing or reviewing your estate plan is to look at your current situation, to know where you are today and to assess what you want to do. An estate plan, like any plan, reflects your situation and what you want to do at the time it is prepared.

Take this quiz. Any "No" or "Unsure" answers may require special attention.

CHECKLIST ✓

Yes No Unsure

❏ ❏ ❏ Have you prepared and signed a will?

❏ ❏ ❏ Have you prepared and signed a financial power of attorney?

❏ ❏ ❏ Is your will and power of attorney for financial matters up to date?

❏ ❏ ❏ If you are married or cohabitating, have you taken steps to protect any assets you brought into the relationship?

❑ ❑ ❑ Have you named beneficiaries and alternate beneficiaries for your RRSPs, annuities, life insurance policies, LIFs and RRIFs, pension plans, and/or DPSPs?

❑ ❑ ❑ Are your beneficiary designations up to date?

❑ ❑ ❑ Have you named a backup executor in your will and back-up powers of attorney?

❑ ❑ ❑ Have you provided for all your dependants?

❑ ❑ ❑ Have you ensured that your spouse will not have to make a claim against your estate?

❑ ❑ ❑ Have you estimated the income tax due on death?

❑ ❑ ❑ Have you left assets to your spouse which can be rolled over tax-free?

❑ ❑ ❑ Have you reviewed how to best register the ownership of your assets?

❑ ❑ ❑ Have you estimated the cost to have your will probated?

❑ ❑ ❑ Do you have enough money to pay the cost of dying— including income taxes and executor and probate fees— without forcing the sale of family assets?

❑ ❑ ❑ If you have specific wishes regarding your funeral, have you left instructions with your executor?

❑ ❑ ❑ Have you prepared a living will or medical directive?

❑ ❑ ❑ Have you prepared a power of attorney for personal care or a health care proxy?

❑ ❑ ❑ Have you documented your wishes regarding organ donations?

❑ ❑ ❑ Have you considered making a planned gift to charity?

❑ ❑ ❑ If you have a business, do you have a succession plan?

❑ ❑ ❑ Does your spouse/children/executor know the names and addresses of your professional advisors?

❑ ❑ ❑ Does your spouse/children/executor know where to find your financial records, income tax returns, bank accounts, safety deposit box, and insurance policies?

❑ ❑ ❑ Have you prepared a personal inventory? (See Chapter 20.)

❑ ❑ ❑ Have you prepared all the necessary documents (including will, living will, powers of attorney) for your estate plan?

❑ ❑ ❑ Do you have all the information required to complete your estate plan?

❑ ❑ ❑ Is your estate plan up to date?

1

WHAT IS ESTATE PLANNING?

"If she'd only known ... and done something about it!"

J.

Estate planning is probably the most difficult area of financial planning for people to focus on. Estate planning is about providing for others—your family, your business partners, charity—and deals with the final chapter in your life.

If you find it difficult to deal with the questions that need to be considered and the decisions to be made surrounding your own death, you are not alone. But consider that these decisions are related not to *if* but rather to *when*. One woman told me, "This is so difficult for me to think about, and to be sure I'm making the right decisions. But I don't want the government making these decisions for me or my family." It's amazing how keeping the government out of one's personal affairs is a powerful motivator.

The Top Five Reasons for Not Preparing an Estate Plan

1. You like to pay taxes.
2. Your family always gets along.
3. The government will look after it for you.
4. You're not old enough.
5. You will live forever.

Estate planning can help ensure the desired outcomes for your beneficiaries on your death. You don't need to be rich to do estate planning. Anyone with a few assets and a family has an estate. Your estate consists of everything you hold or own title to, such as your home, bank account, stocks, bonds, mutual funds, real estate, business interests, pension plans, insurance policies, car, jewellery, art and coin collections, and other personal items. Whatever the value of your estate, simple steps can help to ensure that who you want to benefit does.

The plans you create will reflect your current situation and what you expect will be necessary for the future. However, you cannot predict the future, so it is likely that you will need to update your estate plan as time passes. At a minimum, an estate plan requires preparing or updating the appropriate documents.

WHAT SHOULD BE IN AN ESTATE PLAN?

An estate plan should reflect your family situation, your current and future income needs, your investment strategy, your current assets and debts, and any business interests. At times, estate planning is a balancing act between your objectives, your family dynamics, and legislation. But your will and your total estate plan need not be complex. Indeed, some of the best estate plans are straightforward, if not simple. Estate planning is really a personal matter, and what works for one person may not work for you.

One of the keys to an effective estate plan is to be as straightforward as possible so your executor, beneficiaries, and trustees don't have to guess at what you intended.

Traditional estate planning is the process of taking stock, making decisions, considering the special needs any beneficiaries may have, and preparing the appropriate documents for the orderly transfer of your assets to your beneficiaries.

There are essentially four ways to distribute your assets:

1) according to the intestate rules of your province if you die without a will

2) according to the instructions in your will

3) by giving them away prior to your death, and

4) through joint ownership of property.

Option one is a default option—it comes into effect if you fail to plan and prepare a valid will. Regardless of the simplicity or the sophistication of your estate plan, estate planning requires preparing a will. Depending on your circumstances, you may require option three or four in addition to a will to effectively distribute your assets. But estate planning is much more than the distribution of assets.

A proper estate plan addresses all of the issues relevant to your personal situation and priorities, and could include

• meeting your financial needs for the rest of your life

• protecting yourself in case you become unable to manage your own affairs

• documenting who will receive what after your death

• appointing your executor to administer your estate

• providing direction to your family regarding your wishes for medical treatment, organ donation, and funeral arrangements

• ensuring that your family will be able to manage financially after your death

• choosing who will look after your children

- protecting the interests of the children from a previous marriage
- planning so that your business survives without you
- saving your estate thousands of dollars in fees and income taxes
- ensuring that your beneficiaries receive the full value of their inheritance as smoothly as possible
- planning charitable donations.

In addition to questions related to "what do I want to happen when I die?" there are questions related to "what if something happens to me before I die?" that require additional documents, what I refer to as "pre-estate" documents. Pre-estate documents, such as powers of attorney and living wills, can be powerful additions to a traditional estate plan. These documents can help ensure that appropriate decisions are made on your behalf if you are unable to decide for yourself. They address such questions as:

- Who will look after your finances?
- Who do you want to make health care decisions for you?
- What health care decisions do you want them to make?

Most married women will outlive their husbands, so part of your estate plan may include ensuring that your partner (or yourself) is prepared to manage the money. Even today, managing the money tends to fall in the male's domain. Part of estate planning may include introducing your spouse to your advisors and familiarizing him or her with the types of investment decisions that need to be made. And you want to make sure that there will be enough in the estate or from insurance to maintain your family's lifestyle.

WHEN SHOULD YOU PREPARE AN ESTATE PLAN?

Some people think they are too young to do estate planning. Yet age is not the main factor. We all hope to live to a healthy old age; not all of us will. As soon as you have some assets or a family, you should have an estate plan. Estate planning is not something that you do at the end of the day. Rather, it should be part of your ongoing financial strategy. People in their late forties bury their friends, people who were in their peak earning years who hadn't stopped to consider that they may be mere mortals. Despite all our medical and technological advances, we cannot escape death. Now this does not mean that we should live in paranoia. It just means that every once in a while you should imagine what would happen if you were suddenly not in the picture. And take the appropriate measures.

Like any financial plan, your estate planning requires periodic tune-ups to keep it effective. If you marry, remarry, divorce, or are widowed, a review of your estate plan may indicate that changes are needed to reflect your new personal circumstances. If the people appointed in the will are unable or unwilling to act on your behalf, the documents should be updated. If your assets increase or decrease in value, the amount of income tax due on your final tax return will change. And importantly, your estate plan should reflect changes in tax legislation, succession law, and family law. If you retire at 65 and live to be 85, that's 20 years of changing legislation and family dynamics.

When it comes to estate planning, it is better to be too early than too late!

DO YOU WANT THE GOVERNMENT TO BE ONE OF YOUR BENEFICIARIES?

Governments are waiting for you to die—so they can collect those final income taxes. Now that the $100,000 capital gains exemption has been eliminated, your estate could face higher income taxes than ever before. The tax planning side of estate planning can help keep more for your beneficiaries, reduce your taxes, or provide a higher income for yourself in your retirement years.

Even Canadians who do not consider themselves wealthy by traditional standards have accumulated significant wealth during their lifetime. People who are now 60 or more were taught to be savers. They also invested in property—property whose values rose rapidly through periods of high inflation. (You may remember when houses cost $10,000!) The values of personal real estate and other assets have increased the net worth of more than one generation of Canadians. Surveys reveal that more disposable wealth is about to change hands in the next two decades than ever before.

If leaving a large estate is not one of your priorities, you might look at ways to reduce the size of your taxable estate. You might spend more money today on yourself or give some away. Take your RRSP (Registered Retirement Savings Plan) or RRIF (Registered Retirement Income Fund). We have been taught that it is better to leave money in these registered plans for as long as possible. So let's say you are 62 and your husband dies. You transfer his RRSP to your own (tax free) and let it grow for another seven years until you are 69. At that time you start taking out the minimum amount allowed, and then you die at age 75. What happens, simply stated, is that approximately half of your registered plan is collected as income tax by Revenue Canada. An RRIF worth $150,000 when you die, where there is no surviving spouse, will have a tax bill of about $75,000. Of course, you want to be sure that you have enough for your needs, but do you really want the government to be a major beneficiary? I'm not advocating that you run out and spend all of your RRIF, but you may want to see if the tax bill can be minimized.

IS IT WORTH PREPARING AN ESTATE PLAN?

Governments are becoming more invasive in our personal lives, and legislation concerning transfers of property, taxation, and family law is increasingly complex. If you do not plan your estate, the government has legislation to protect your interests. But the rules the government follows may not reflect your family relationships and how you want your assets distributed. You may not want some bureaucrat making decisions on your behalf. You may just want to make sure that your family does not have to report to some government official to justify their actions.

Having seen what happens when people do not have a current will, I don't believe that anyone over 18 with a family, a bank account, a house, or just a few personal possessions can afford *not* to write a will.

How estate planning can keep more money for your beneficiaries:

$ minimizes taxes

$ leaves enough cash to pay your bills

$ minimizes probate fees

$ schedules charitable gifts

$ prevents your children from spending their inheritance prematurely

$ designs income splitting techniques

$ protects your assets from creditors

$ ensures that your business doesn't die with you

Some people say, "Why bother? Let the kids look after themselves." I think, in some cases, this is an attempt to avoid looking into the future, to face mortality. There are many questions to be asked and decisions to be made when you develop an estate plan; some are for the benefit of your beneficiaries, but some are also for you. If thinking about your own mortality seems morbid to you, think of the alternatives.

Through estate planning, you can speak for yourself and for your family when you are no longer able. And with proper advice you can keep from making business, legal, investment, or tax blunders.

In addition to the dollars you may save by planning your estate, the financial plan can provide a sense of security. It can give you that peace of mind that comes from knowing that you have looked after your financial affairs in the best possible way. John F. Kennedy said, "There are risks and costs to a program of action. But they are far less than the long-range risks and costs of comfortable inaction."

You don't do estate planning for yourself—you do it for others. Although it may be too much to expect, an effective estate plan could also reduce family tensions. We all know stories where brothers and sisters no longer speak to each other because one feels that the other received some unspoken advantage. The result of a successful estate plan is the preservation of your assets (from taxes or a forced sale) *and* the smooth transfer of those assets to your beneficiaries in a manner that satisfies your wishes.

I interviewed S., aged 66, a few years after the death of her husband. He had never been particularly interested in handling the family finances, so she was used to dealing with their money. At the time of his death, the family assets were registered either in her name or in both names and his will reflected his current wishes. On his death, the assets were transferred smoothly and with a minimum of expense. Her words of wisdom: "Educate yourself! Get advice! And use common sense!"

2

WILL THERE BE ANYTHING LEFT?

"It is better to live rich than to die rich."

Samuel Johnson

For some people, retirement and estate planning go together. But I have said before, I believe that estate planning is important at all ages.

Planning your estate does not mean you should concentrate on building as big an estate as possible for the benefit of future generations. Like some people, you may not be overly concerned about providing your children and grandchildren with a big inheritance. You may even have one of those bumper stickers that says "I'm enjoying my children's inheritance!" You've probably worked to provide for your retirement, not theirs. But many people in their forties and fifties are hoping to receive an inheritance as part of their own retirement planning!

Your first priority in estate planning should be to ensure that you have enough to meet your own income needs. Some people have been taught to be good savers and have developed a large estate but do not know how to wisely spend what they have. Often when I ask couples in their late sixties how much income they need to live on in a year, they don't know! They just spend as little as they can and worry about money all the time. Traditional estate planning assumes that you will have money or property at the time of death and looks for effective ways to distribute that money and property to your beneficiaries. As we will see, there are a number of ways to reduce taxes when you are planning your estate (see Chapter 9 for a fuller discussion). But let's not forget that one way to reduce the amount of tax that is due on death is to give some of your estate away while you are alive or to spend some of it yourself.

Before you adopt either of these strategies, figure out what you'll need to live on throughout your retirement so that you don't outlive your money. Sometimes an elderly person is afraid that she will not have enough money to see her through old age when there is, in fact, more than enough money. Or I talk with the children of an elderly parent who wants to give away some of his money today as part of his tax and estate planning, but the children are concerned he may not have enough money for the future. If you give away too much today and later on find that you require additional money, you may not want to ask your family to support you at that time.

RETIREMENT PLANNING

As our governments cut costs and social benefits, we need to become more responsible for our own retirement. We expect that the social benefits, such as Canada Pension (CPP) and Old Age Security (OAS), will not be so generous in the future, if they even exist. The real issue though, is not whether there will be enough Canada Pension or seniors benefits or company pension to provide for you in your retirement, but what do you see yourself doing when you are 55, 65, or 75? Studies show that 85% of Canadians are not saving enough for the retirement lifestyle that they want. So what will be there for an estate?

Ideally, at some point in your life you will make the transition from *creating* a nest egg to living off the nest egg. I'm often asked "Is it enough?" and "How long will it last?" Without knowing the answer to these questions, you may worry that you will outlive your money. No one can tell you exactly how much you require or how long it will last. But a retirement income projection, based on experience and some conservative assumptions about the future, can give you some guidance. Even though retirement projections are just projections, they are useful in determining if you are on track, or what changes you might need to make in your planning. A retirement income calculation, or projection, should consider

• your current income

• an estimate of the annual income you want throughout retirement

• the age at which you would like to retire, or your current age

• life expectancy statistics

• the monthly income available from all sources at retirement (including CPP and other seniors benefits if you assume that they will be available)

• the value of your current RRSP savings

• the value of your savings and investments outside your RRSP

• assumptions regarding inflation and annual returns on your investments.

T I P A retirement projection could help you determine if there will be enough for your own needs—with maybe something left over.

Thirty years ago people spent less time in retirement. Back then a man who retired at 65 spent an average of seven years in retirement. Statistics Canada tells us that a man retiring today will live until he's about 80. If he retires at 65, that's 15 years in retirement. But if he retires at 55, it's 25 years in retirement. And a woman retiring at age 65 can expect to live to 84 on average.

With the number of years spent in retirement increasing, prudent financial planning does not end at retirement. No longer can you do retirement planning at age 65 and expect the world to stay more or less the same for the next seven years. It is important to stay abreast of changes in legislation and tax rules as well as economic trends. Retirement and estate planning can help keep more for yourself and for the next generation.

A CASH FLOW ANALYSIS

One technique you can use to assess your financial situation is writing a budget that looks at your sources of income and your day-to-day expenses over a month or a year. It answers the immediate question, "Do I have more coming in than I have going out?" but it doesn't give you a perspective on what your financial situation might be in a few years.

> **T**
> **I**
> **P**
>
> Look for ways to cut your expenses without cutting back on your lifestyle. Don't be proud. If you qualify for discounts and benefits based on your age, apply for them! If you travel outside Canada, even for a day, make sure you have adequate health insurance coverage. Falling ill outside Canada and having to pay uninsured medical bills can substantially eat into the value of your estate.

A cash flow analysis is a better way to assess ways to maximize your income and reduce your taxes over more than one year. It is similar to the types of assessments businesses do of their financial health. A cash flow analysis considers your various sources of income and your expenses year by year. It should also consider the effects of taxation and the financial decisions you might make during retirement. It should help you to determine which sources to draw from, such as early CPP and early conversions from RRSPs to RRIFs, and when. Income sources could include

- a company pension, and whether it is indexed to inflation
- CPP benefits
- OAS or seniors benefits at age 65
- Guaranteed Income Supplement (GIS) for lower-income individuals
- investment income

- income from registered plans, RRSPs, Life Income Fund (LIF), and RRIFs
- income from an annuity
- business income
- Workers' Compensation Board benefits
- War Veterans allowance
- alimony or maintenance payments
- rental income
- income from the sale of a home
- trust income.

How you structure your income in retirement will affect the value of your estate at the time of your death. For example, if the investments in your RRIF earn more than the amount withdrawn, the value of your RRIF will continue to grow. The cash flow analysis will also project the value of your estate for each year.

The cash flow analysis also looks at the effect of those questions that begin with "what if" such as

- What if I withdraw cash for a trip around the world?
- What if I convert to a RRIF at 65 rather than waiting until age 69?
- What if I withdraw more than the minimum payout from the RRIF? Or if I withdraw only the minimum?
- What if I start CPP at age 60 rather than 65?
- What if I have to go into a nursing home at age 80?
- What if interest rates are lower in the future than they are today?

By asking the "what ifs" you may be able to identify opportunities to maximize your income and minimize your taxes over a number of years. Just by rearranging their current finances, one couple was able to keep 10% more of their annual income in their hands by sending less to Revenue Canada. Take CPP as an example. If you and your spouse are over 60 and retired, you could split your CPP benefits, so you each receive an equal benefit. If you are entitled to $8,000 and your spouse is entitled to

$2,000, you can split the benefits so that you each receive $5,000 per year. If this strategy would reduce your tax bill, contact your local Income Security Program of Human Resources Development Canada (see the blue pages of your telephone book) for the necessary forms. By sending Revenue Canada only what is required each year, you might live a little more comfortably or have your nest egg last a little longer.

> Beware of a cash flow analysis where the assumptions are overly optimistic. A cash flow analysis is only a projection. There are no guarantees that the future will unfold as we assume. And so the cash flow analysis should be reviewed periodically to reflect any changes, such as your income requirements, updated assumptions, and changes to the tax rules and government benefits.

INCREASE YOUR INCOME THROUGH A REVERSE MORTGAGE

If you are a retired homeowner, you may wish to stay in your home. But what if you also have a shortage of income? One of the newer options available in Canada to supplement your income is the reverse mortgage, which can provide you with a regular income, secured by the equity in your home. There are a number of options and features available with reverse mortgages. It is recommended that you obtain professional advice to ensure that you understand how a particular reverse mortgage agreement works.

In a regular mortgage, you make monthly payments of interest and principal to eventually pay off the mortgage. In a reverse mortgage, the monthly income you receive is obtained by tapping into the value of your home and advancing it to you. The equity in your home is reduced by the money advanced to you and the interest charged.

It takes years to pay off a regular mortgage when you borrow to buy a home. A reverse mortgage works in the reverse direction. When you borrow from the equity in your home and are not required to repay the principal or the interest, the power of compounding works against you and your estate. This makes some people uncomfortable, especially those who do not believe in debt, or believe that a debt should be paid off as quickly as possible. But, if all your money is tied up in real estate *and* you need income, a reverse mortgage can provide it.

Reverse mortgages are not for everyone, and you should ensure that you understand all of the terms, and the implication of the terms, in the contract. There is a good book on this topic called *Have Your Home and Money Too!* written by P.J. Wade and also published by John Wiley & Sons.

COMMON DEATH BENEFITS

A number of death benefits may be available to your estate, depending on your age, family situation, and work history. Don't forget to consider these benefits when calculating what amounts are available to your spouse and dependants after your death.

CANADA PENSION PLAN

CPP payments stop at the time of death. But CPP pays a lump-sum death benefit and monthly survivor benefits to those who apply and meet the criteria for eligibility. The amount of the lump-sum death benefit is based on the number of years the deceased paid into the Canada Pension Plan and how much was paid. In 1996 the maximum lump-sum benefit was $3,540.

In addition to the lump-sum payment, two types of monthly pensions are available:

• a monthly survivor pension to the deceased's spouse

• a monthly orphan benefit to children of the deceased (they may still have one living parent)

If the deceased contributed to Canada Pension for only a few years, the actual amount of any monthly benefit will be less than is shown in the table below.

	Maximum Amount
Survivor Spouse* Benefit If spouse is over 65	$436.25 monthly

Survivor Spouse* Benefit
    If spouse is between 45 and 65 or
    under 45 and disabled or
    under 45 with dependent children
	$399.70 monthly

Survivor Spouse* Benefit
    If spouse is under 35, not
    disabled and there are
    no dependent children
	none

Child Benefit
    If child is under 18 or
    between 18 and 25 and at school
    full-time
	$164.17 monthly

*or common-law spouse

The deceased did not have to be receiving CPP benefits at the time of death, but these benefits are *not* paid out automatically. Appropriate paperwork needs to be completed and proof of death submitted before any benefits are paid. Forms are available from the local Income Security Program office and some funeral homes.

Your spouse or executor should file the paperwork for CPP benefits with the Income Security Program office promptly after death since there is a one-year limit on any monthly benefits. For example, if your survivors apply 18 months after your death, the monthly payments can be made retroactive to a maximum of 12 months. Applying 18 months after death would mean losing 6 months of benefits.

Any benefits received from the Canada Pension Plan are taxable. The monthly orphan benefit is considered the child's income, and if it can be saved in the child's name, any income earned on it is taxed at the child's (presumably) lower tax rate. The lump-sum death benefit can be included on the income tax return of either the beneficiary or the estate. The executor will determine which tax return to use so that the lowest amount of tax is paid. (Tax returns for the deceased are discussed in Chapter 10.)

CPP survivor benefits end on the death of the surviving spouse or when the spouse no longer qualifies. Orphan benefits stop when a child is too old to qualify or stops attending school. But if a child leaves school and then returns, and is still under 25, he or she can apply to have the benefits reinstated.

OLD AGE SECURITY

OAS payments stop on death. Although OAS does not pay a death benefit, a surviving spouse might receive monthly spousal OAS payments if he or she meets the income and residency tests.

WORKERS' COMPENSATION

If the death is due to a work-related disease or disability, a lump-sum payment or ongoing monthly payment may be available from the Workers' Compensation Board.

WAR VETERANS ALLOWANCES

If the deceased was receiving a War Veterans allowance, he or she may qualify for funding to pay for the funeral, cremation, or burial expenses. For more information, contact your local Veterans Affairs Canada office.

Where the estate cannot afford a dignified funeral and the deceased veteran meets wartime service and income tests, the estate may be eligible to receive funds to pay for the funeral through the Last Post Fund.

COMPANY PENSION PLAN

The rules for employee pensions vary from company to company. The following highlights some of the benefits that may be payable under your company pension plan. I recommend you read your employee benefit statement or contact the benefits person in the human resources department of your current employer and/or former employers to find out the details of any death benefits available and the details of any group life insurance still in force.

If You Are Not Retired

A company pension plan may pay a death benefit to your beneficiary. The benefit might be

- a lump sum based on the contributions made into the plan while employed, plus interest
- a lump sum based on an actuarial calculation, or
- a deferred pension benefit.

There may also be some vacation pay and unpaid wages to be collected.

If You Have Retired and Are Receiving a Pension

Many spouses assume that they will continue to receive their spouse's company pension after their spouse dies. I've seen the devastation when a recent widow calls her spouse's former employer and finds out that his pension died with him. When you die, will your spouse continue to receive your company pension? The answer to this question could make a huge difference to whether your family will have enough to live on after your death. And if your pension will stop on your death, sit down with your spouse *now* and figure out what can be done.

Depending on the pension option you select at retirement, the monthly pension could

- stop on the death of the retiree
- continue to the beneficiary to the end of a minimum guaranteed period, such as 5 or 10 years after retirement. For example, if you retired late in 1991 and the guaranteed period for your pension payments was 10 years, and you happen to die in 1999, your surviving spouse would continue to receive pension cheques until late 2001.

- continue to the death of the surviving spouse, if you elected a joint survivor pension option. In exchange for taking a lower monthly benefit at retirement (sometimes as much as 40 % lower depending on the age of your spouse), the company pension agrees to pay the pension until the death of the surviving spouse. With this option, if you outlive the retiree, the survivor pension would last as long as you do.

Even though the monthly amount under the joint survivor option is lower than under some of the other pension options, it is often not in a spouse's best interest to sign away the right to this option. Some advisors question whether a spouse should even be able to sign away the right to a survivor pension. However, the survivor option might not be necessary if the spouse has his or her pension plan or substantial independent means, or if the estate is *guaranteed* to have enough assets or life insurance to provide an income to replace the pension. Before signing away the right to a survivor pension, your spouse should obtain independent financial and legal advice.

OTHER BENEFITS

If you have purchased an annuity, the death benefit, if any, depends on the payment period chosen. For a "life only" annuity, the payments end on death. If there is a guaranteed period, such as "5 years" or "15 years" under the annuity contract, the annuity payments will be paid to the named beneficiary until the end of the annuity contract. For example, if the guaranteed period was for 10 years, and you die at the end of year 8 of the payment period, then the payments to the designated beneficiary continue for two years.

SUMMARY

Calculating if you or your spouse will outlive your money is not an exact science. We cannot anticipate future changes to the income tax rules or other legislation or the value of the Canadian dollar or the costs of health care. Estimates need to be made based on some assumptions:

- how much money you require to maintain your standard of living
- how long you will live
- the rate of return your investments will earn
- the inflation rate
- the future costs of such things as retirement homes

I recommend erring on the side of having too much money at the time of death, rather than too little and keeping a cushion of money beyond what you think will be needed.

Any plan should be reviewed every couple of years or so to ensure that it reflects your priorities and needs as well as changes to the relevant legislation. Economist Peter Drucker said, "The best way to predict your future is to create it."

It should be clear from the discussion of benefits that could be available that your estate is not just something everyone else has to deal with after your death. The choices *you* make concerning your financial situation before and after retirement mean the difference between taking care of your loved ones and saddling them with financial difficulties on top of their grief.

3
DYING INTESTATE: DISTRIBUTING YOUR ESTATE WITHOUT A WILL

"Facts do not cease to exist because they are ignored."
Aldous Huxley

When it comes to estate planning, too many people think in terms of "if" rather than "when." Maybe this helps to explain the results of a 1993 survey conducted for the Trust Companies Association of Canada that found that only half of Canadians over 18 have a will.

Someone who dies without a valid will (or one that can be located) is considered to have died intestate—without a last will and testament. Governments were quick to realize this is one area that could eventually affect everyone. So your provincial government has statutory rules that lay out who gets what and other rules for those who die without a will. The distribution of assets according to these rules could have nothing to do with what your beneficiaries need or how you would have liked your estate to be handled.

Some people assume that their assets will go to the government if they die without a will. This is not true. The government is only the beneficiary of last resort and is sometimes called the "ultimate heir." Assets will go to the government only if you die without a will *and* have no living relatives, a process called escheat. (Why does it have the word "cheat" in it?)

Let's take a look at what happens if you die without a will.

WHO GETS WHAT

Under the provincial statutory will, assets are distributed according to your province's intestacy rules. There is no flexibility in these "one size fits all" rules. People *you* want to benefit may be left out, and those who do benefit may not be whom you would have chosen. If you have a family member that you would like to receive a little extra to cover a special situation, the statutory rules do not make allowances. If you have a common-law spouse, he or she is not entitled to receive property under the intestacy rules in most provinces. If you have children from a former marriage, your assets could end up in the hands of your current spouse's children, rather than your own.

If you have a spouse and young children, your intentions may be like many others'—to have your spouse receive your entire estate, and then on his or her death, to have any remaining assets distributed to your children. But it is incorrect to assume that if you are married all your assets will automatically go to your spouse. Most provinces have a preferential share, ranging from nothing to $200,000, that your spouse is entitled to before any assets are distributed to your children.

Table 1 lists the preferential share in the provinces, not including Quebec.

TABLE 1

Province/Territory	Preferential Share*
Alberta	$40,000
British Columbia	$65,000
Manitoba	$50,000
New Brunswick	$ 0
Newfoundland	$ 0
Northwest Territories	$50,000

Nova Scotia	$ 50,000
Ontario	$200,000
Prince Edward Island	$ 50,000
Quebec	$ 0
Saskatchewan	$100,000
Yukon	$ 0

*as of January 1996

Your spouse will receive the entire estate after all the debts are paid only if you have no children or the value of your estate is very small. If your estate is worth more than the preferential share and you die intestate, your spouse will *not* receive your entire estate and part of your estate will go directly to your children! While this may be appropriate in certain circumstances, it is not always.

If you do not have a will and you have no surviving spouse or children, your estate is distributed to other family members.

Table 2 shows the distribution of the residue of an estate for someone who died without a will. The residue of an intestate estate is what remains of the estate after all taxes, bills, fees, and expenses have been paid.

TABLE 2

DYING INTESTATE WHEN THE VALUE OF THE ESTATE IS GREATER THAN THE PREFERENTIAL SHARE (PROVINCIAL SUMMARY)

Surviving spouse with

no children	Spouse receives 100% of residue.
one child	Spouse receives preferential share of residue. If no preferential share, or for amounts over the preferential share, half of residue goes to spouse, half of residue to child.
more than one child	All provinces except Manitoba: spouse receives preferential share, if there is one, plus one-third of the remaining residue. Children share remaining two-thirds of residue.

> *Manitoba:* spouse receives prefer-
> ential share plus half of the
> remaining residue. Children share
> other half of residue.

No spouse

   one or more children Children share residue equally.

   no children   Parents share residue equally.

No spouse, no children,

   no parents   Brothers and sisters share residue
                      equally. If no brothers or sisters
                      are living, then all nieces and
                      nephews share residue equally. If
                      no distant family can be found,
                      estate goes to the provincial gov-
                      ernment.

Some provinces have laws that protect a spouse's interest in the family home or the estate even if someone dies intestate. For example, if you die intestate in Ontario, your spouse can make an election under the *Family Law Act* to receive no less than 50% of the net family property (see Chapter 11). In Manitoba, the *Homestead Act* protects a surviving spouse's interest in the family home.

If a will does not distribute some part of an estate, the distribution of that part is handled according to the provincial intestacy rules. For example, a will drafted without the assistance of a lawyer might miss wording to distribute the residue. In that case, the residue would be handled according to the intestate rules.

Table 3 shows the distribution of an intestate estate in Ontario. We will use this information in the two examples that follow.

TABLE 3

DYING INTESTATE IN ONTARIO

Survived by a spouse* with

   no children   Spouse receives 100% of residue.

   one child   Spouse receives first $200,000 of
                       residue. If residue is greater than

	$200,000, half the excess goes to spouse, half to child.
more than one child	Spouse receives first $200,000 plus one-third of residue over $200,000. Children share remaining two-thirds of residue.
No spouse	
one child	Child receives 100% of residue.
more than one child	Children share residue equally.
no children	Parents share residue equally.
No spouse, no children,	
no parents	Brothers and sisters share residue equally. If no brothers or sisters are living, then all nieces and nephews share residue equally. If no distant family can be found, estate goes to the Ontario government.

Spouse according to Revenue Canada includes a common-law spouse. Spouse under the Ontario Succession Law Reform Act refers only to married spouses.

Let's look at what happened to John and Joan, who lived in Ontario.

EXAMPLE

John and Joan were married for 25 years. They had two children, Robert, 16, and Elizabeth, 19. John and Joan had a mortgage-free house worth $150,000 that was registered in John's name, $100,000 in life insurance with Joan named as the beneficiary, and $200,000 in stocks, bonds, and GICs in John's name. John had always been too busy with business to prepare his will, and he assumed that Joan would receive everything. Besides, he was only 49 and thought there was lots of time.

John died suddenly, without a will. His assets were distributed as follows:

The life insurance was paid directly to Joan because she was the named beneficiary on the policy.

The rest of his estate was distributed according to the intestate rules in Ontario.

Total value of the estate: $350,000

Joan was entitled to the first $200,000 of the estate, so she received the house ($150,000) and $50,000 of the investments.

Of the remaining $150,000 in investments, Joan was entitled to one-third and the children shared the remaining two-thirds, so Joan received an additional $50,000.

Elizabeth received her share of the $50,000 immediately; the $50,000 for Robert was held by the public trustee and was paid to him when he turned 18.

You may say this distribution is fair because it gives the teenagers money to complete their education. But what if they used it to buy cars and travel? Could Joan have managed the family money to provide for her needs and the needs of the children without involving the public trustee for Robert?

Change the numbers in the above example and see how they might work for your situation. Do your provincial intestate laws reflect your family's needs and your wishes? Most people, when they understand what will happen under a statutory will, write a will, or plan to write a will, or start to think about planning to write a will.

When Revenue Canada started treating common-law spouses the same as married spouses for tax purposes, people reasoned this meant that common-law spouses were treated the same as married spouses under *all* legislation. Not true. Common-law spouses do *not* receive automatic rights to property under intestate law. They may have rights to the matrimonial home or financial support if they were financially dependent on the deceased, depending on provincial family laws.

EXAMPLE

Tom had left his wife, Terri, two years ago and had set up housekeeping in an apartment with Mary, who had her own career. Tom and his wife never divorced or legally separated. Tom's will named Terri his executor and the sole beneficiary. What happened on his death? Terri received everything.

If Tom had done some estate planning, he might have handled it differently. When he first thought about planning, he'd been living with Mary only for a few months and he didn't want to formalize a new estate plan until he was sure the relationship would last. Well, time slipped away and he never got around to it, which left Mary out in the cold.

If you are in a same-sex relationship, none of the current intestate or succession laws help. To ensure that assets or property go to your partner, you must formalize an estate plan through a will, a contract, a trust, life insurance, or jointly owned property. I wish I could say that you could rely on the good will of other family members, but that is not normally the case. The family may not be aware of the relationship or may not be supportive of it. From what I've seen, legal entitlement usually overrides any humane considerations.

COURT-APPOINTED ADMINISTRATOR

Without a will, no one can manage the deceased's affairs until an administrator is appointed. No one has the authority to act until the court appoints the administrator to distribute the estate according to the intestate rules; the administrator is given powers similar to an executor's and the authority to administer the estate. Generally, the court issues Letters of Administration or a Certificate of Appointment of Estate Trustee Without a Will (similar to Letters Probate—see Chapter 7) to family members in a priority list that starts with your spouse, children, and grandchildren. The person appointed may not be anyone you would have picked, or even the most suitable family member to do the job. (In some provinces, this person is called a personal representative.)

Everything is held in limbo until the administrator is appointed. Look at your own situation and ask yourself, "What would happen to my assets or business if no one had the authority to make decisions and to carry them out for a period of time?" Consider the stress this could place on the family. If the deceased was married, his or her spouse will likely suffer from the uncertainty and the wait—both of which could be avoided if there had been a will.

The Canadian population is growing older and governments are cutting back their services. For those of you who don't bother to write a will, I hope this is one government department that will continue to have enough resources to process all of the paperwork for your family!

DELAYS IN THE DISTRIBUTION OF YOUR ESTATE

With a valid will, your executor receives the authority to act as the administrator of your estate as soon as the will is confirmed through a process called probate. Without a will, expect it to take longer for your estate to be distributed to your beneficiaries.

HIGHER COST OF ADMINISTERING YOUR ESTATE

The cost of administering an estate without a will is higher than the cost of administering a similar estate with a will. Additional costs may include

- legal fees for your family to apply to the courts to have an administrator named

- the cost of posting a bond to ensure the assets in the estate are not mismanaged by the administrator or if the executor is not a Canadian. Bonding is an expense not normally required for a Canadian executor named in a will. This financial bonding may be obtained through an insurance company (for an annual premium).

- additional legal fees to settle other issues.

The couple of hundred dollars it costs to write a proper will is a lot cheaper than the hundreds or thousands of dollars it can cost to settle an intestate estate! One lawyer I know will not even estimate the cost of settling an estate when there is no will until he knows the people involved and the financial situation of the deceased.

ADDITIONAL INCOME TAXES PAYABLE

Most people merely resent the amount of income taxes they pay while they are alive—but they would be livid if they understood the potential tax bill they face on death. If you did not prepare a will, then you probably did not look at the whole area of estate planning. As a result, your estate can end up paying more income taxes than would have been the case if you had done some planning.

As we have seen, if you have a spouse and children, your spouse does not automatically receive all of your assets. All assets left to a spouse can be rolled over on a tax-deferred basis to that spouse. But any assets received by your children are considered "sold" by Revenue Canada, with no ability to defer taxes. If those assets have increased in value since you acquired them, your estate will end up paying additional income tax.

Sometimes, skipping a generation and leaving assets to your grandchildren in trust (such as for their education) can result in a lower overall family income tax bill. But this strategy cannot be accomplished without a will.

LOST INVESTMENT OPPORTUNITIES

Without a will, no one has the legal authority to manage and renew your investments until an administrator is appointed by the courts. In one family, a brother died and a surviving sibling watched the value of shares owned by the deceased drop from $25 to $5 per share over five weeks. No one had the legal authority to step in and issue instructions to sell those shares before the price hit bottom. The deceased was only 33—and had not yet considered any estate planning.

Once appointed, the personal administrator has limited investment powers and may only hold investments listed in your province's *Trustee Act*. There is nothing inherently wrong with this list, yet an investment might need to be sold when market conditions are less than favourable, unless special court approval is obtained (more fees!). It also means your administrator cannot consider investments that might otherwise have fit into your investment strategy. With a will, you can give your executor the powers to manage your investments as they see fit.

APPOINTMENT OF GUARDIANS

A guardian is someone who looks after a child until that child reaches the age of majority. Legal documents refer to children as minors, but they are anything but a minor consideration. In fact, providing for children motivates many people to prepare their first will.

If you have children under the age of majority (which differs by province), and die without a spouse and a will, the courts will name a guardian for them. The person appointed by the courts may not be someone you want to assume this role for your children. However, the public trustee (also called the official guardian or children's lawyer) will consider the recommendations of your relatives.

UNDERAGE BENEFICIARIES

An inheritance paid to a child has to be held in trust for that child (unless the court instructs otherwise) until he or she reaches the age of majority *even* if you have a spouse. To protect the inheritance, the trustee may be required to report to the public trustee periodically and account for how money was spent and managed on behalf of the children—not something a parent normally has to do. If a large sum of money is involved, the trustee may also be required to post a performance bond for the money.

Alternatively, the assets might be administered by the public trustee of your province.

Minor beneficiaries are entitled to receive their share of the intestate estate when they reach the age of majority. Remember when you were 18? How would you feel about your children receiving a lump sum of money at that age? You may want to ensure that their day-to-day living and education requirements are provided for but that they not receive a large sum until they are older (and presumably more mature). Unfortunately, without a will the inheritance cannot be held longer, even if distributing it later better meets the children's needs.

NO PROVISION FOR JOINT DISASTER

Some couples assume that if they own their house and hold all their assets jointly, they do not require a will. But joint registration does not provide any protection if you and your spouse die together—in a common disaster.

If spouses die in a common disaster without a will, the property of each is distributed as if each had died before the other. His property is left to his beneficiaries and her property is left to her beneficiaries.

SUMMARY

The choice is yours. Prepare an estate plan, including a will, or use the provincial plain vanilla "one size fits all" version. If your estate is distributed according to the intestate rules, it will likely face more legal fees, lengthy delays, and higher income taxes, not to mention the additional aggravation to your surviving family. I'd rather have a will (and do!) that distributes my assets as I see fit, gives my executor some flexibility, is tax effective, does not require reporting to the government, and has any money for my children managed by people who know what is important to me.

Now that you know, have you made an appointment with a lawyer to prepare your will?

4
DISTRIBUTING YOUR ESTATE THROUGH A WILL

"I went to the lawyer, signed my will, and got on the eleva-tor to go home. The elevator got stuck between floors and I was sure that I was going to die then and there because my will had just been prepared. After what seemed like hours, but was really only minutes, the elevator doors opened and I crawled up to the nearest floor. My friend, who was wait-ing in the car, said I looked like I'd seen a ghost." M.

Are you one of those people who have put off preparing a will because you feel that writing down your wishes will short-en your life? Contrary to what you may think, writing a will does not result in a premature death! Yet many people find it difficult to think about preparing a will, let alone talk about it.

A will is the cornerstone document of an estate plan and has two main functions. The first function is to appoint an executor to administer your estate. The executor is sometimes called a trustee, personal representative or personal administrator. The second function is to document how your assets are to be dis-tributed to your beneficiaries. Having a will makes settling your estate more straightforward and less expensive than if you die without a will. You are free to leave your assets and property to whomever you wish and exclude certain people from receiving any benefits, subject to family law in your province.

Through a will you can

• appoint an executor to look after administering and distributing your estate

• assign specific administrative powers to your executor

• specify how you want your estate managed and distributed after your death

• decide who gets your money and assets

• indicate your choice of guardian for your children and establish a trust for any assets to be held for them until they are older

• distribute your assets in such a way as to minimize your final income taxes

• implement strategies to reduce income taxes that are not possible without a will, and much more.

A will is a signed legal document that can be revised and updated as often as necessary. The instructions in your will come into effect only on your death. Until then, they have no effect.

Q. *I've prepared my will and have left my grand piano to my niece. If I need money, can I sell the piano without checking with her?*

A. You are free to sell the piano at any time without the permission of your niece. The wording in your will does not come into effect until your death. If you do not own the piano when the will takes effect, the instructions regarding the gift are just ignored.

The following are samples of estate distributions found in the simplest wills.

1) You have a spouse and children. Your will leaves everything to your spouse, and your spouse's will leaves everything to you. If

your spouse is not alive at the time of your death, everything is to be divided equally among your children. If the children are under 18, everything is to be held in trust until they are 21 or older. Until the children reach 21, their education and living expenses are to be looked after from the money held in the trust. Guardians are named in the will.

2) You have a spouse only. Your will leaves your estate to your spouse, with the condition that if your spouse predeceased you, your estate is left to the alternative persons or charities named.

3) You have no spouse or children. Your estate is left to the persons or charities of your choice. If a person named is not alive at the time of your death, then the residue is left to the alternative persons or charities named.

Even simple instructions may take seven or eight pages to express them in the legal jargon! And not all wills are so simple. Depending on the situation, a will can be very lengthy and complicated.

> Keep the instructions in your will as simple and straightforward as possible. Even though you might be tempted, don't try to rule your assets or your family "from the grave."

When you plan your will, consider a number of "what if" scenarios and add the appropriate instructions in case they occur. "What ifs" might include:

• What if your spouse predeceases you?

• What if you and your spouse die together?

• What if you have more children?

• What if one of your children predeceases you?

• What if the main executor is unable to do the job when required? Who should act as your backup?

Preparing a will often requires a fair amount of consideration to determine how you wish to have your estate handled and who will receive what. Many people tell me they are surprised at the amount of time and thought that planning a will can take. Often the hardest decisions are who will be the executor and the guardian.

You can do just about anything you want in terms of your bequests, although there are some restrictions. For example, if you are supporting family members and you do not adequately provide for their support and maintenance, they can apply to the courts for continued support from your estate. In some provinces, spouses are entitled to special consideration. (See Chapter 11 for a fuller discussion of family law.) Failing to address these restrictions could overturn some of the provisions in your will. Be sure to discuss your situation with your lawyer.

Q & A

Q. I do not want to leave my children anything. Can I leave them out of my will?

A. You can't write a will that says "my spouse and children get nothing." If you try, family law allows those who are financially dependent on you to challenge your will.

To prepare a valid will, you must be mentally competent and either:

- have reached the age of majority in your province, or
- if under the age of majority, be married or a member of the armed forces or a mariner.

Lawyers usually make notes regarding your mental competency at the time your will is prepared. This is done by confirming that you know the nature and extent of your assets, understand the legal implications of making a will, know the people or organizations that will benefit under the will, and understand your family situation. In most cases, someone in the advanced stages of Alzheimer's disease or other mentally debilitating condition will not be able to prepare or revise a will.

A lawyer who has doubts about your competency may request a doctor's note to confirm that you are of sound mind at the time the will is drawn up. If unable to confirm your mental competency, the lawyer will not be able to prepare your will. A will successfully contested on grounds of incompetency is ruled invalid and will result in an intestate estate, or the estate being settled by a previous will if one exists.

If someone is mentally competent but death is imminent, a lawyer can come to the bedside to document the instructions. It may be wise to have them discuss their wishes privately with the lawyer, to avoid undue influence from family members, business associates, or friends.

Although much of this book looks at estate planning from your own personal perspective, if you have parents who have not yet prepared their wills, I urge you to help them get to their lawyer. I am not suggesting that you should know the contents of their wills—it can be a confidential document until after death—just see that they have prepared their wills.

WHO GETS WHAT

A person or organization that benefits under a will is called a "beneficiary." Money or property that a person receives through the instructions in a will is sometimes referred to as a gift, a legacy, or a bequest.

Some people have goals that include building an estate so that they can leave significant assets to their beneficiaries. Some people feel no need to leave a large estate and intend that the beneficiaries will receive only whatever is left over. You need to determine what is appropriate for your situation and fits your beliefs.

A will can deal with the assets and property you own but it *cannot* deal with those assets that have other legal ways of being distributed on your death, such as

• jointly held property (registered in more than one name)

• business assets that are dealt with under a shareholders' agreement or buy-sell agreement

• RRSPs, RRIFs, and pension plans where a beneficiary is named at the financial institution

- income that you receive from a trust, where that trust agreement states that the income ceases on your death. For example, you are receiving income from a spousal trust, set up in your late husband's will, where the trust states that on your death any remaining assets are to be distributed to the children from his first marriage.

- assets that are dealt with in a written marriage contract.

If there is someone whom you wish to exclude from your estate, you can write them out of your will, unless that person is your spouse or is financially dependent on you. For example, if you are estranged from your adult son and he does not require the inheritance, you could leave him nothing in your will. However, I suggest that you consider carefully before doing this. More than one estate has been held up for years, during which none of the beneficiaries received any benefits, because the estranged child did not feel fairly treated in the will.

Understand that people left out of the will may not be happy. It may be useful to specifically mention your reasons in your will, or in a letter that you file with your will. If the will is challenged, or contested, and ends up in court, the letter, while not legally binding, will explain your intentions and provide guidance to your executor or the courts. I recommend that you leave such individuals something, however small, so that it would be difficult for them to contest your will on the basis that you had made an oversight.

Q. *I have two daughters, one of whom I have not heard from in 10 years. Must I divide my estate between them?*

A. No. You are free to decide who you leave your estate to. You might want to leave a nominal sum to the absent daughter so that you do not leave her out entirely.

If you suspect that your will might be challenged, you could place your assets in an inter vivos trust while you are alive (see Chapter 13) and distribute them through the trust agreement rather than the will. Sometimes, talking the situation through with a trusted person can help you determine what you feel in your heart you should do. Then talking to a professional can help you determine how to do it.

Q & A

Q. I've been left out of my father's will. What can I do about it?

A. Before disputing the will's contents, consult a lawyer. Disputing a will can be an expensive proposition. If you were financially dependent on your father, you may be able to make a claim against the estate for support. Otherwise, if the will is valid and drawn up properly, you may be out of luck.

Your children and grandchildren may be referred to as your "issue" in a will. In the event that one of your children predeceases you, consider how you would like your estate distributed. Options include leaving the bequest to their children, allocating their portion to your other children, or naming an alternative beneficiary.

One option is to make the inheritance to your children "in equal shares per stirpes," sometimes called the grandchild clause. Per stirpes means that if a child predeceases you, the gift that would have been theirs passes to that child's children (your grandchildren). A less common method to pass gifts on to the next generation is to make the inheritance "in equal shares per capita." Per capita means that the inheritance will be divided equally among your children who are alive at the time of your death.

Let's look at the difference between per stirpes and per capita in a real-life situation.

EXAMPLE

You have three children who each have two children of their own.

WORDING 1:

The will states that $90,000 is to be divided in equal shares "per stirpes." One of your children dies in a car crash before you. On your death, the $90,000 will be distributed as follows:

Child A $30,000
Child B $30,000
Child C $30,000 is left to C's two children

WORDING 2:

The will states that $90,000 is to be divided in equal shares "per capita." One of your children dies in a car crash before you. On your death, the $90,000 will be distributed as follows:

Child A	$45,000

Child B	$45,000

Child C	$	0.	C's children are not included in this distribution.

In this situation, the grandchildren (children of child C) may already be having a tougher time of it because they have lost a parent. You want to be sure you don't cut them out of your will just because of a technical wording. If you don't want C's surviving spouse to have access to the grandchildren's money, this can be ensured through additional instructions in your will (and selecting a suitable trustee to manage the money).

REDUCING THE COST TO DIE

In addition to who gets what, attention should be paid to the tax implications. How do you keep Revenue Canada from getting more than their fair share?

EXAMPLE

Mr. Goderich has a wife, 62, and an adult son. He and his wife own their house free and clear. His other assets include a $300,000 life insurance policy and a $150,000 RRSP. He has named the beneficiaries as follows:

On his life insurance policy, two-thirds of the death benefit to spouse, one-third to son.

Resulting distribution:	wife receives $200,000; son receives $100,000.

On the RRSP, two-thirds of the value to spouse, one-third to son.

Resulting distribution:	wife transfers $100,000 directly to her own RRSP; son receives

	$35,000 ($50,000 less withholding tax).
Total to wife:	$300,000
Total to son:	$135,000, since $15,000 was immediately lost to Revenue Canada.

If Mr. Goderich wants to leave one-third of his estate to his son, he could name his beneficiaries as follows to send less to Revenue Canada:

On the life insurance policy, half of death benefit to spouse, half to son.

> Resulting distribution: wife receives $150,000; son receives $150,000.

On the RRSP, 100% of benefit to spouse.

> Resulting distribution: wife transfers $150,000 tax-free to her own RRSP.

Total to wife:	$300,000
Total to son:	$150,000, since nothing is immediately lost to Revenue Canada

Mr. Goderich should determine how his wife will manage financially after his death, since she has never worked. One suggestion is to leave her all the assets, since his son (ideally) has a whole lifetime of employment ahead. But Mr. Goderich was concerned she would spend it all and nothing would be left for his son. Maybe some of the funds could be held in a trust for Mrs. Goderich so that she could use the income (and maybe a little of the capital) each year until her death. Then whatever is left would go to the adult son. If too much is left to the son, Mrs. Goderich could end up financially dependent on him.

MAKING THE GIFT MORE TAX EFFECTIVE

Rather than leaving all of your assets to your spouse, some income splitting between your spouse and your children could be arranged by setting up a family trust, to reduce the overall family tax bill.

EXAMPLE

Jack is leaving a $250,000 inheritance outright to his spouse, Sonna. Some of the money will be used to raise and educate his two children, 8 and 10. Without a family trust, Sonna will be responsible for paying the income tax on any investment income earned.

Income earned on the inheritance:
$250,000 at 10% = $25,000 annually

Since Sonna is in top tax income bracket because of her employment income, the family tax bill on the inheritance will be:

$12,500 annually

But what would happen to the family tax bill if the bulk of the estate is left to Sonna and a trust is set up for the children's expenses and education? If Jack leaves $150,000 outright to Sonna and $100,000 in trust for the children, the overall family tax bill will be lower since the children have little or no other income of their own.

Income earned on inheritance in Sonna's name:
$150,000 at 10% = $15,000 annually

Income earned on inheritance in trust:
$100,000 at 10% = $10,000 annually

Tax bill on inheritance income in Sonna's name (50% tax bracket) will be:

$7,500 annually

Tax bill on inheritance held in trust will be:
$2,700 annually

Total family tax bill on inheritance income will be:
$10,200 annually

Annual tax saving before expenses (when compared with previous scenario) will be:

$2,300

In the second scenario $100,000 is held in a testamentary trust and is taxed at a lower rate than the money left outright to Sonna. Is it worth it? Well, there is a hassle factor related to filing an income tax return for the trust and administering the inheritance separately, and there may be trustee fees, but over the years the tax savings would certainly add up.

WHAT IS FAIR?

When determining who gets what, there is also the issue of fairness. As I tell my children, fair does not necessarily mean equal. It depends on the individual situation. Just as you may wish to leave to family members specific items that have sentimental value to them, you may wish to leave bequests of different amounts to family members. There may be a special circumstance that you want to assist, such as a grandchild who has a special interest in the arts.

What if you do not have a spouse to whom you can roll over assets tax-free? If your intention is to have each of your children benefit equally from your estate, you need to consider how to manage this on an after-tax basis.

EXAMPLE

You have a son and daughter that you want to receive equal benefits from your estate. You have an RRSP worth $100,000 and GICs worth $100,000. You have named your son as the beneficiary of your RRSP and have left your daughter the residue of your estate.

	Market Value	Received by Beneficiary
RRSP left to son	$100,000	$70,000 ($100,000 less $30,000 withholding tax)
GICs left to daughter	$100,000	$80,000 ($100,000 less $20,000 additional tax due on RRSP proceeds)

One way (but not the only way) to deal with this type of situation is to name your estate as the beneficiary of the RRSP (even though this would mean probate fees to be paid) and in your will leave your son and daughter each 50% of the residue of your estate. In the above example, if the beneficiary of the RRSP was your estate, your son and daughter each would receive about $75,000 through the will.

Have you loaned one of your children money that has not yet been repaid? You may want to forgive the loan in your will but still be fair.

Q. I've loaned $12,000 to one of my adult sons and want to forgive the outstanding balance on my death. How can this be handled in my will?

A. First, I recommend that you have your son sign a promissory note, to keep the loan as businesslike as possible. File the note with your important papers. If it is your intention to have your children benefit equally from your estate, you can leave your children equal shares of your estate. Your son with the loan would have his share reduced by the amount of the outstanding balance on the loan.

One man said that when his wife died, everything was left to him. However, his wife had loaned one of their daughters $30,000. When the mother died, the daughter took the balance as a gift since there was no written agreement for the loan. Unable to discuss this with his daughter, the father didn't raise the issue of repaying the loan. However, five years later, the situation still bothers him. If only she'd said, "Dad, I'll continue making the payments to you now," or at least "Thank you."

YOUR EXECUTOR

One function of your will is to appoint an executor who is responsible for managing and distributing your assets according to the instructions in your will. The executor has a long list of duties related to the estate and wrapping up the deceased's personal affairs.

RESPONSIBILITIES OF THE EXECUTOR

An executor's responsibilities include

1) arranging the funeral. Make sure that your family and executor are aware of specific requests or instructions you have regarding your funeral arrangements. You may want to write a letter to your executor stating your wishes. Although oral or written instructions regarding the funeral are not legally binding, your executor will normally follow your wishes. On the practical side, sometimes the instructions are found after the fact and your executor cannot carry them out!

2) acting as trustee and managing the assets of the estate for the benefit of your beneficiaries. After your death, one of your executor's responsibilities is to locate your assets and property and transfer the ownership from your name to your estate. For example, the ownership of a brokerage account might be re-registered as "The Estate of Joan Smith." If required, your executor must probate the will (see Chapter 7). Ensure that your executor knows the location of your current will, personal inventory, and important papers. The more information you can provide your executor with, the better he or she can ensure that all of your assets are found and handled properly.

3) settling the bills of the estate, including all legitimate claims by creditors, funeral expenses, and other expenses.

4) filing the final tax returns for the deceased and the estate on time and ensuring that any income tax owing is paid. Before all the assets of your estate can be distributed, your executor should obtain a clearance certificate from Revenue Canada to confirm that all income taxes have been paid.

5) distributing assets and property to your beneficiaries according to the instructions in your will.

Q & A

Q. I've been named in a will as a beneficiary. When will I receive my inheritance?

A. To some degree, that depends on who the beneficiaries and executors are. Technically, the residue of the estate cannot be paid out until:

- After income taxes, funeral costs, debts, and the trustee fees are paid.
- The clearance certificate has been received from Revenue Canada unless the executor wants to be personally liable for any income taxes and penalties that may be due.
- Any family law requirements have been met.

POWERS OF THE EXECUTOR

The executor gets his or her power from the will. If the extent of the executor's powers are not specified in a will, they are defined in your province's *Trustee Act*. The powers assigned in the will can be as broad and extensive as appropriate for your situation or as limited as you see fit. Additional powers could include

- power to distribute assets, in kind or as is, to beneficiaries (legally called "in specie")
- power to sell assets and pay cash to beneficiaries
- power to purchase assets of the estate
- power to provide some funds to the family before the estate is completely settled
- power to make an RRSP contribution to a spousal RRSP
- authority to pay taxes before the assets of the estate are distributed. If there is income tax due, you may wish to indicate that the residue of your estate be responsible for paying these taxes.
- power to make elections under the *Income Tax Act* that would be beneficial to your estate but are beyond the powers stated in the provincial *Trustee Act*
- power to determine if and when assets are to be sold
- power to invest as they see fit. If your executor is a trust company, will you give them the power to invest in their own securities (such as a mortgage they arranged)?
- power to determine which assets, if any, are to be held in a spousal trust

- power to borrow on behalf of the estate
- power to consult with or hire professionals, such as accountants, lawyers, professional trustees, or financial advisors, and to pay them from money in the estate.

Sometimes executors are reluctant to hire professionals because they see it as spending the beneficiaries' money. For example, an executor might attempt to sell the house privately to save the estate the real estate commission. Unless the executor is familiar with the local real estate market, this might result only in a lower selling price for the house and no additional profits for the beneficiaries.

APPOINTING YOUR EXECUTOR

Your executor is named in your will. You are allowed to appoint more than one executor (co-executors) if you feel that better decisions would be better made by two executors or that the job is too complex for one person. You should also appoint a back-up executor in case your first executor predeceases you.

The person you select should be someone you trust completely and who has the financial and business sense to manage and distribute your assets. Someone who has never completed an income tax return may not be the best choice. If your assets include a business, ideally that person should understand the business. It also makes sense to select someone who lives relatively close to where the estate needs to be administered. Also consider the age and health of your executor; you are looking for someone who will be around when you—or rather your family—needs them.

Your executor may be your spouse, another family member, a professional trustee, or a close friend. A family member may best understand your family circumstances. If your spouse is the primary beneficiary of your estate, it often makes sense for the spouse to be named as executor, if they are able to manage the responsibilities. If you have no spouse, you might appoint another family member or a close friend.

If it is not appropriate to appoint your spouse, you might appoint your children as co-executors. (However, this is not advisable as a technique to try and bring your children closer together.) Before naming your adult children as the executors of your estate, consider:

Yes No Unsure

❑ ❑ ❑ Are they capable of managing the financial responsibilities of the estate? Look at how they manage their own credit cards and financial affairs.

❑ ❑ ❑ Are they willing to accept the job?

❑ ❑ ❑ Do they have time to do the job?

❑ ❑ ❑ Can they handle the responsibilities fairly and objectively?

❑ ❑ ❑ Do they live in your province?

❑ ❑ ❑ If you are considering having them act as co-executors, do they get along well enough to be able to work together to make the necessary decisions?

If you've answered "no" or "unsure" to any of these questions, carefully consider if you want to name your children as co-executors. In some cases, it might be better (and easier for everyone involved) to appoint one child as the executor and to leave a note for the other children explaining your reasoning.

If you anticipate struggles for control of assets or a business, if you know no one who has the expertise to be your executor, if no one is willing to accept the job, if the assets are to be held in trust for a number of years, or if your financial and family affairs are complex, you may be better off appointing a professional executor, such as a trust company, an accountant, or a lawyer. It may not be fair to family members to have to deal with all of this.

Q. *My spouse and I each have one child from our previous marriages and one from our own marriage. Whom should I appoint as executor?*

A. There is no simple answer. Look at whether the children get along. Are you setting up a spousal trust? How are the assets to be distributed? The greater the family tensions, or the possible family tensions, the more useful a professional trustee may be.

Some people feel that appointing a family member to work with a professional executor is a good solution since a family member understands the family situation and the professional can handle the administrative and legal requirements to get the job done. If you decide on a co-executor arrangement with a professional executor, you can appoint the primary decision-maker or you could indicate that they are responsible for making major decisions jointly and that the professional trustee is responsible for the administration.

Q & A

Q. Should I choose a trust company to be my executor?

A. The majority of wills appoint a spouse or family member as executor. But depending on the complexity and the value of your estate, you might want to consider a professional executor, especially if

- there are business income, foreign property, and many types of investments in the estate
- family members may not be able to act impartially
- a trust created in the will is expected to exist for many years—longer than you want to impose on friends or family
- you feel that family or friends could not handle the job.

According to a survey conducted by the Trust Companies Association of Canada in 1993, fewer than a third of Canadians who had written a will had discussed its contents with the executor they had named. Talk to the person or people you would like to name as executor, or have already named, and be sure that they are willing to assume the role. Review with them any special instructions contained in your will.

If they have never acted as an executor, they may not be aware of the responsibilities of the job. If *you* have never acted as an executor, you could both talk to someone who has to learn more about what is involved. You may both be surprised at the amount of work that the job can entail—and to find out that an executor who loses any of the estate's money can be held personally responsible. (If your spouse is the executor *and* the main beneficiary of your estate, this may not be an issue.)

Just in case your first choice for an executor predeceases you or is unable to do the job when required, you should name a back-up executor. If you don't, and your executor predeceases you, the executor of *their* estate may end up handling your estate too! If you don't appoint an alternative, your estate must apply for letters of administration (in Ontario, this is now called the Certificate of Appointment of Estate Trustee Without a Will)—leaving no one to manage your estate until a court appointment.

Q. *We've updated our wills and power of attorney documents. We have two sons in their forties. Our eldest has his own paralegal firm and we've made him the executor of the estate. Have we made a mistake by not naming both of them?*

A. It seems that you are comfortable with your eldest acting as executor for the reason you stated. You could speak to your youngest son and discuss your decision with him. If that is not practical, you may want to write him a letter that explains your reasons, and file it with the will. Have you treated them equally in the distribution of your assets? That's where it really matters!

COMPENSATING YOUR EXECUTOR

Your executors, whether they are family members or professionals, are legally entitled to receive compensation out of the estate (before the residue is distributed) for their services. The fee amount is established by legislation in some provinces. Executor compensation appears to be around 3% to 5% of the value of the estate, but to some degree it depends on the time required to administer the estate. The courts have frowned on executors charging fees based solely on the value of the estate and not related to the actual effort involved. Family members, especially if they are beneficiaries, rarely charge trustee fees when acting as the executor, unless administering the estate is particularly time-consuming.

Trust companies have their own minimum fees for administering an estate. In early 1996, one trust company's trustee rate schedule was:

on first $250,000 of the estate	4.75%
on next $750,000	4%
on balance over $1 million	3%

Q. It is expected that at the time of my death, my estate will be valued at $800,000. How much might it cost to have my estate administered by a trust company?

A. Using the above rate schedule, trustee fees would be:

on first $250,000	$11,875
on next $550,000	$22,000
Total	$33,875

If these fees seem high, discuss with the professional trustee what services will be involved. These could include estate planning, preparing the will and a personal inventory, ongoing consultation, as well as administering the estate after death. Trustee fees may be negotiated when you are selecting your executors. Lower fees may be charged for administering your home passing through the estate, or where the trust company currently manages your accounts.

KEEPING YOUR WILL UP TO DATE

Just as having a will is important, it is also important to keep your will current. There are no statistics to tell us how many wills are currently up to date. But from what I've seen, many are not. They don't reflect what people want to have happen and they don't reflect changes in personal circumstances and legislation.

You may update or change the instructions in a will in one of two ways: by drafting an entirely new will or by amending your will using a "codicil." A codicil is a formal amendment that is attached to the will and requires the same number of witnesses as the will. It is generally cheaper to prepare a codicil than an entirely new will, but ask your lawyer. You may be surprised to find that in some circumstances, there is not much of a cost difference. Writing a new will automatically revokes the older will. Destroying a will also revokes it.

To update your will, *do not* write on it. While it may seem simple, for example, to cross out one name and replace it with another, doing so can invalidate that clause in your will.

Q. How do I know if I should use a codicil or prepare a completely new will?

A. As a rule of thumb, if a codicil would make your instructions complicated or unclear (maybe because it refers to a number of clauses in the will), then preparing a new will might prevent confusion or ambiguity. If you have moved to a new province, you may also want an entirely new will. If you are making major changes to the way your assets are to be distributed, you might indicate your reasons in the codicil so that the changes would be more difficult to challenge.

Once the new will is prepared, signed, and witnessed, old wills should be destroyed to ensure that your estate is not mistakenly settled with the wrong will. This has happened! In one instance, an executor had an original will and settled the estate on that basis, unaware that a newer will existed.

Don't destroy an old will until the replacement is signed and witnessed! If you die in between, you die intestate.

Reviewing your will periodically is not just an exercise in morbidity or a way to provide your lawyer with more fees. From time to time, review the contents of your will to ensure that it still documents your intentions and reflects current legislation, and that all named parties (executor, guardians, trustees) are still willing and able to perform those duties. Circumstances change. Family members come and go, you could marry, be widowed, divorce, start a family, or move, to name a few. (See the checklist "Considerations When Reviewing Your Will" at the back of this book.)

Moving

Estate planning is governed mainly by provincial legislation, and the rules vary from province to province. If you have moved to another province, review your will in light of that province's laws. In some provinces, spouses have rights to the matrimonial home and to no less than if you had divorced. If you fail to address these minimum requirements in your will, these rights could override the distribution in your will. As well, you should determine if it is still practical for your executor to handle your estate.

Q. I have a will that was written in Texas. Is it valid in B.C.?

A. Your will is still valid. However, you should review it with a lawyer in relation to the laws of British Columbia. At a minimum, if your executor lives in Texas, bonding may need to be posted and he or she may find it difficult to settle your estate due to the distance involved. There may also be issues related to the residency of the trust for tax purposes. You may want to name a new executor who lives closer to your assets.

Legislation Changes

Legislation related to estate planning, succession law, trusts, taxation, probate, and family law changes periodically. Professionals can best help you assess the impact of such changes on your estate plan.

Marriage and Remarriage

Marriage and remarriage automatically revoke a will, unless, in most provinces, the will specifically states that it was drawn up "in contemplation of marriage." If you do not write a new will after marriage and then you die, you die intestate unless your spouse elects to accept the old will. But how likely is that if your new spouse is not named in the will? If you don't prepare a new will, expect to die intestate!

If you are contemplating marriage or have recently married, your will needs to be reviewed. (Or prepared if you do not have one.)

> **If you are preparing a will in contemplation of marriage, consider wording that makes any bequests to your future spouse dependent on the marriage actually taking place.**

If you remarry and have children from a previous marriage, you may want to make special plans to provide for them. The simplest will that spouses can prepare, the mirror will (where spouses leave everything to each other, and then when you both are deceased, leave everything to the children), would leave your children dependent on the wording in your new spouse's will.

And if you have a new spouse, you can take advantage of the tax-deferred rollover on an RRSP or RRIF by naming him or her as beneficiary.

SEPARATION

As long as you are legally married, you cannot write your spouse out of your will unless you have a marriage contract stating otherwise. However, if you prepare a separation agreement, you likely will want to write a new will. If you are supporting any children, ensure that you have made adequate provision for the support to continue in the event of your death, so that it is less likely that your estate will be challenged.

DIVORCE

If you divorce, a will prepared prior to the divorce is not automatically revoked, but a couple of provisions in the will are affected.

- Any asset or bequest left to your now ex-spouse is revoked.

- Your ex-spouse cannot act as executor, so your estate would have to apply to the courts to have an executor appointed.

On divorce, review your will. Chances are your intentions have changed. In my opinion, you should write and sign a new will at the same time as the separation or divorce agreement is written and signed. If child support payments are required according to the divorce agreement, make sure that you have adequately provided for the support to continue after your death. And if you wish to name your ex in your will, you'll need wording to the effect that this is what you want even though you are divorced.

Also review the beneficiary designations on your pension plans, life insurance, RRSPs or RRIFs, and keep them up to date.

Keep a photocopy of your will so you can refer to it and review its contents at any time.

SUMMARY

The contents of your will do not need to be disclosed to anyone (other than your lawyer) while you are still alive. I recommend that you tell your executor and your family, or at least your spouse, the details of your financial affairs and where your documents, accounts, and the like are. In an ideal world, everyone would discuss with their executor and family how their assets are to be distributed, but it is often difficult for families to be open, especially when it comes to finances and death. If you are able to discuss your will with your family, they may better understand and appreciate your decisions. At a minimum, ensure that someone in your family and your executor know where to find your will and the list of all your assets and liabilities (see "Personal Inventory" at the back of this book) and wishes for organ donation and funeral instructions. A will may not be seen until after the funeral.

Your will is an important legal document. If the original of the will cannot be found, then the courts will assume you died intestate.

Q. *Where should I keep my will?*

A. In a safe place. Treat it as the important document that it is and make sure your executor knows where it is. You might leave your will

- with your lawyer (who would hope to assist your family with the administration of your estate)
- in a safety deposit box if someone has the authority to access the box after your death, otherwise, the box may be sealed on death, making it difficult to access
- with your other important papers at home
- with the provincial estates office, or
- with a trust company if you have decided that you require a professional executor.

A will is only one of the ways you can distribute your estate. Assets and property can also be distributed while you are alive, beneficiaries can be named on RRSPs, RRIFs, and life insurance, inter vivos trusts and joint ownership can be used—these can all be part of estate planning.

5
THE FORMAT OF A WILL

"Get black on white."

Guy de Maupassant

A will consists of a number of clauses, like paragraphs, that specify your instructions. Some wills are long, with pages and pages of instructions. Others require only a few pages. The shortest will I've seen was a military will that was just one page—but it contained only a bare minimum of instructions.

Although the format of a will varies from will to will, lawyer to lawyer, and from province to province, a few standard clauses are normally included. Each clause needs to be clear and precise, with the correct legal wording so the instructions can be accurately followed when the time comes.

The sample wordings in this section are not legally complete and are *not* to be used to prepare your own will. They are included so you can better understand the purpose of a clause or phrase when you read a will. Since a will reflects an individual's personal situation, it may contain some unique clauses that are not described in this chapter.

COMMON CLAUSES

IDENTIFY THE TESTATOR

A formal will begins by identifying the person writing the will by name, address, and sometimes occupation at the time the will is prepared. A will is a document that cannot be shared; each person requires a separate will to document their own wishes.

REVOKE ALL PREVIOUS WILLS

The first clause states that this will is the *last* will and testament and revokes all former wills. This clause is included in almost every will as a precaution, even your very first will. If a second will is found, everyone will know to follow only the instructions in the most recent will.

APPOINT YOUR EXECUTOR

Appointing an executor is one of the two main purposes of a will. A clause names your executor and gives him or her any additional powers required to manage your estate. The will should also name a backup, or alternate, executor in the event that the first executor is unable or unwilling to perform the duties when required.

Q. My father just died. His will was written in 1968. The only person he named as his executor died three years ago. What happens now?

A. The first person asked to replace a named executor would be the backup named in a will. Since there is no backup named in your father's will, the courts will look next to the executor's executor—that is, the person named in the *executor's* will. If that person too is deceased, I expect that your lawyer will need to ask the courts to appoint someone to take on the responsibilities. If your father had only updated his will!

AUTHORIZE YOUR DEBTS TO BE PAID

To ensure that the executor has the legal authority to pay your debts from the estate, including funeral bills and income taxes, there is normally a clause in the will to this effect. If you do not authorize your debts to be paid, don't think that you can avoid them; creditors would place claims on the estate to ensure they got paid, and that could delay the distribution of assets to beneficiaries.

Paying debts normally takes priority over the distribution of assets indicated in the will.

SPECIFY WHO GETS WHAT

Next come clauses specifying who gets what, which may be in the form of a specific gift or bequest, or as part of the residue clause. These are the instructions beneficiaries are most interested in.

Make Any Specific Bequests

A specific bequest in a will gives the beneficiary something outright, such as "I leave my brother, Edward Scott, $10,000" or "I leave $5,000 to charity X." There are many types of bequests, each with a slightly different wording.

Type of Bequest	Sample Wording
Gift of a specific sum of money	"I give A the sum of $___."
Gift of a specific asset	"I give B my collection of___."
Contingent gift (dependent on conditions)	"I give___to C only if my spouse does not survive me."

A will may contain many specific bequests, or none. If there are no specific bequests, the assets of the estate are distributed according to the residue clause in the will.

Distribute the Residue

The residue is that part of the estate that remains after all taxes, debts, fees, and expenses are paid and specific bequests made. To ensure that a will deals with all the deceased's assets and property, it should contain a clause indicating how the residue is to be distributed. In some wills, all of the estate is distributed as part of the residue clause. In other wills, the residue distributes only what is not otherwise bequested.

The clause to distribute the residue might read "I give A 30% of the residue of my estate and B 70% of the residue" or "I leave my spouse, C, 100% of the residue of my estate."

If the residue clause is missing, part of the estate could be distributed according to the intestate rules.

OPTIONAL CLAUSES

A number of additional clauses can exist in a will, depending on your family situation and your wishes. Some lawyers include these as standard clauses.

APPOINTING A GUARDIAN FOR MINOR CHILDREN

A guardian is someone who assumes the responsibility for a child until that child reaches the age of majority. If you are a single parent, or in the event that you and your spouse are killed in a common disaster, you should appoint a guardian for your children. Hopefully, the person named as guardian in your will is never called on to do the job.

The guardian you name is granted temporary guardianship for your children. To obtain permanent legal custody, the guardian must apply to the courts. Although the court is not legally required to appoint the guardian named in a will, it generally does unless there is a valid reason not to. If your children are old enough to express their concerns and opinions, the courts may ask them what they would like before a final decision is made.

If you have strong wishes regarding whom you would like to be appointed as guardian for your children, or strong wishes regarding whom you would *not* want to be appointed, indicate that in your will and state your reasons. It could help the court make a decision that is in the best interests of your children.

Q. *The guardian I appointed in my will has died and now my will needs to be updated. Can I just write in the name of the new guardian?*

A. No. Writing on a will invalidates that clause. If the rest of your will is up to date, prepare a codicil to document the change and have it properly signed and witnessed.

Discuss your needs with the person you want to appoint as guardian to ensure that he or she is willing to take on this responsibility. If you have numerous children of various ages, you may want to consider if it is practical for them to stay together. You may also want to leave the guardian a lump sum of money as a token that you appreciate that they have stepped into this role on your behalf. Raising one's own children is difficult; raising someone else's is noble.

Ask yourself these questions when you are selecting your children's guardian.

Yes No Unsure

❏ ❏ ❏ Is the person someone your children would want to live with?

❏ ❏ ❏ Is that person willing to assume the responsibilities as their guardian?

❏ ❏ ❏ Can that person afford to raise and support your children?

❏ ❏ ❏ Does your will provide financial support for the children while they are in the guardian's care?

Any "no" or "unsure" answers require special attention.

From time to time, check with the guardian or guardians appointed in your will to ensure that they continue to be willing and able to take on the responsibility.

Managing Assets for Minor Children

Assets that might be left to underage children need to be held in trust for them until they reach the age of majority. If you have young children, you will need a clause naming a trustee to manage those assets their behalf. If you do not name a trustee, the public trustee is required to step in until the children reach the age of majority. If the children's guardian or surviving parent needs money for the children's benefit, a formal application has to be made to the public trustee. Government agencies are not known for their quick responses to requests for funds.

If you do not want your children to receive the assets as early as age 18 or 19, you can have wording in your will to restrict payment until they are older and, presumably, more mature. Some parents restrict a lump-sum payment until the children reach 23 or 25, with access to the funds earlier for education expenses. (See Chapter 13 on trusts.)

Q. Can my children's guardian and the trustee of my children's money be the same person?

A. Technically, yes. However, if a large amount of money is involved, there could be a perceived conflict of interest in managing the assets on behalf of the children's needs versus the guardian's own needs.

Common Disaster Clause

One of the "what ifs" to consider when writing a will is what happens if you and your spouse are killed in a joint disaster, or if your entire immediate family dies in a car crash. Lawyers usually add a survivorship clause describing how your estate is to be distributed in the event that you and your spouse die simultaneously (this is usually defined as within a certain number of days of each other).

Unless your will states otherwise, the distribution of your estate will be based on who died last. If it is determined that your spouse survived you, then all your assets and your spouse's assets would go to your spouse's family; if you survived your spouse, all the assets would go to your family. To benefit both families equally in this event, you and your spouse could each document that in the event of a common disaster, half of the assets go to your family and half to your spouse's family. Some people also add a charitable bequest in the event of a common disaster when they would rather the money go to charity than a distant relative. This clause also eliminates the need to probate the same assets twice in a short time.

Alternatively, the will might state that a beneficiary must survive you by at least 30 days (or some other period of time) before that beneficiary can receive any benefit from the estate.

INVESTMENT POWERS OF THE EXECUTOR

If a will does not give the executor additional powers related to investments in the estate, the executor is able to invest the money held in trust in the investments that are listed in the provincial trustee legislation. The following investments are allowed in Ontario, for example:

- federal, provincial, and municipal government securities
- first mortgages for real estate in Canada
- guaranteed investment certificates of any trust company or bank
- bank deposits
- term deposits in a credit union
- corporate bonds where the corporation has paid a dividend that meets the minimum requirements
- corporate shares (preferred and common) where the dividend payment meets the minimum requirement.

Sometimes these investments are discussed in terms of restricted, or safe, investments versus unrestricted investments. The list of investments is designed to restrict an executor from speculating with the money held in trust. "Safe" doesn't mean the same things to all people, and in some cases it can mean settling for investments that produce lower returns. But if the assets are in the estate only for a short time, this is not likely a major concern.

In the will, you might want to give your executor a broader range of allowable investments, or unrestricted investment powers. Be aware that there is the potential for abuse when the investments are unrestricted. If your executor is comfortable dealing with money and you trust him or her not to speculate on some wild get-rich-quick scheme, you may want to assign additional investment powers. But if your executor has minimal investment experience, the more conservative route may work best. You could restrict the powers of the executor to a list more limited than the above, but, from a practical point of view, I don't see why you would want to.

Mutual funds are not expressly referred to in most trustee legislation, but this is currently under review. Interestingly, a 1994 court ruling in Ontario suggests that if you want your executor or trustee to be able to hold mutual funds in an estate, you should explicitly authorize the use of mutual funds in your will. If you have concerns about the risks in some specialty mutual funds, you could limit the types of mutual funds by establishing a written investment strategy for your trustee. This is particularly important if you take advantage of the professional management and diversification available with mutual funds.

In my own will, I want my executor and trustee to be able to follow an investment strategy that will provide the greatest benefit to my beneficiaries for both their short-term and long-term needs.

ALTERNATE BENEFICIARY FOR LIFE INSURANCE

If you have life insurance, you may wish to include a clause in your will naming an alternate beneficiary for your policies just in case the primary beneficiary predeceases you. For example, in the event that your spouse dies before you, you may want to name your children, a charity, or your estate as the alternate.

If the conditions related to the alternate beneficiary are complex, include the details in your will. For example, if the insurance death benefits might be left to underage children, you should write into your will instructions regarding holding the money in trust on their behalf. When a beneficiary for life insurance is not properly worded in a will, probate could be required for a life insurance death benefit.

ESTABLISHING TESTAMENTARY TRUSTS

Testamentary trusts, which are set up after death according to instructions in your will, can be used to manage assets for minor children, split income, or save some income tax. The will defines the powers of the trustee, how the testamentary trust is to be managed, and when the assets will be distributed. (For a discussion of testamentary trusts, see Chapter 13.)

HELPING YOUR CHILDREN PROTECT THEIR INHERITANCE

Let's assume that the purpose of your estate planning is to preserve your assets for the succeeding generations in your family. Given the high divorce rate in our country, what can you do to ensure that in the event your son divorces, the inheritance will flow to your grandchildren and not to your son's ex-spouse?

In most provinces, an inheritance is not considered family property, that is, assets and property divided on divorce. In Ontario, the will can include wording to indicate that any growth or income resulting from the inheritance is also not to be considered family property. Alternatively, you might establish a testamentary trust. (See Chapter 11 on family law and Chapter 13 on trusts.)

Your adult children should also prepare their own wills.

HANDWRITTEN, FORMS, AND FORMAL WILLS

Wills can be handwritten, filled out on a preprinted form, or drawn up by a lawyer (or a notary in Quebec).

A will written completely in your own handwriting is called a holograph will. Where a holograph will is recognized, the *entire* will must be in your handwriting and be signed at the end by you. No witnesses are required. But because no witnesses are required, a holograph will may be contested on grounds of incompetency and charges of undue influence by another person. It may be necessary for your executor to prove that the will is in your handwriting. Legal wording, clauses, and appointments that are normally found in a formal will may be absent or incomplete, leaving a handwritten will open to interpretation and legal challenges.

Preprinted will forms are available from many stationery stores and computer software also exists. Caution is required to ensure the will is complete and reflects your wishes. Since this type of will is not written entirely in your own handwriting, formal witnessing is required.

A formal will is normally drawn up by a lawyer. When you pay a lawyer to prepare your will, you should receive more than their wordprocessing capabilities. A lawyer should provide you with legal guidance. The lawyer will take your instructions and prepare the will containing the clauses and wording to meet your needs. The will is then signed by you, in front of the witnesses.

I always recommend a formal will drawn up by a lawyer to ensure that the wording and the provisions in the will are complete and valid. It is an unfortunate fact of life that our laws are getting more and more complicated. Handwritten and preprinted wills are prone to error. You do not want your will to be contested on a technical detail that would result in it, or parts of it, being invalidated. Dying with an invalid will means you die intestate. For example, if the will does not dispose of the whole estate because it has no instructions for the residue of your estate, part of your estate could end up being distributed as if you had died without a will!

A badly prepared will could lead to an expensive court dispute by your beneficiaries—much more expensive than the cost of preparing a formal will. Depending on your lawyer and the complexity of your will, the cost of preparing a will for uncomplicated estate ranges up to $500 plus GST. If you are having a will prepared for yourself and your spouse at the same time, the fee would be about twice that. To make the most of the time you spend with a lawyer, and possibly reduce the time required with the lawyer, read "Considerations When Writing Your Will" at the back of this book and take this information with you to the lawyer.

Q. *What can I expect if I see a lawyer to prepare my will?*

A. Drawing up a will with a lawyer involves meeting with the lawyer to discuss your situation and requirements. The will is then drafted and revised if necessary. There will be a final meeting to review the will and to formally sign the will in front of the witnesses. The more complex your situation, the more time and expense involved.

SIGNING THE WILL

A formal will must be signed and witnessed in the presence of two competent adults. The witnesses should not be anyone named as a beneficiary in the will or the spouse of a beneficiary named in the will. Any gift made to a beneficiary who witnessed the will is likely to be ignored—since there is a concern that they might have unduly influenced the testator.

To save time and expense after death, some lawyers will prepare an affidavit of execution at the time the will is signed, certifying that the witnessing of the will followed proper procedure.

 Preparing the affidavit of execution at the time the will is prepared means that somewhere down the road, your executor will not have to locate the witnesses to confirm that they witnessed the will being signed.

Knowing that you have prepared a formal will means it is done. You don't have to worry about scribbling a handwritten note and calling it a will just before you leave for a vacation or a business trip.

6

DISTRIBUTING YOUR ESTATE BY GIVING IT AWAY NOW

I'm often asked, by either an elderly person or an adult child concerned that mom or dad may be being too generous for their own good, when someone should look at giving away some of their assets and personal belongings. My view, as I outlined in Chapter 2, is that an individual's first obligation is to ensure that they have enough money for their own needs.

For some people, one of their main financial goals is leaving a large estate for the benefit of their beneficiaries. For others, leaving an inheritance is a secondary goal, or not a goal at all.

The techniques discussed in this chapter are not appropriate for everyone. Some make sense for the more senior person who does not require all that they currently have, even if they live to be 100. Some of the strategies are more appropriate closer to death. As well, gifting assets should be done with professional financial advice to be sure that you don't trip up over any income attribution rules or give away too much. No one should give away so much that they end up living in poverty. Determine what you need and set aside an additional cushion for security first.

There can be some advantages to giving away some of your estate while you are alive.

- You can see those people or charities appreciating your generosity.
- Probate fees may be lower.
- Executor fees may be lower.
- You may enjoy the feeling that you have put your affairs in order.
- Your future income taxes may be lower.
- Some gifts may create charitable receipts so you can maximize the tax savings.
- You (and the recipient) may have more privacy.
- Your family may even squabble less after your death!

There are four main disadvantages to giving assets away during your lifetime.

- You might give up the exclusive control over the asset or property (which may be a significant concern if it is a home, business or cottage).
- If the "gift" has increased in value since you acquired it, Revenue Canada may consider that you have "sold" the asset at fair market value, increasing your income tax in that year (unless you gave the gift to your spouse).
- You may continue to be responsible for the taxes on any income earned on the asset under Revenue Canada's attribution rules.
- If you give away too much too soon, you may become financially dependent on others, such as your family or social assistance.

Now I'm not suggesting that you should, or should not, give away some of your money or assets. You must first assess your requirements, for now and in the future. If you are satisfied that your own needs will be met, then give with open eyes. You may want to discuss with the recipient any hopes that you have for how the gift will be used. It is sad when I see the disappointment of someone who gives money to a person who is not at all grateful, or is reckless with the gift.

To give assets, cash, or property, you must be mentally competent and give the gift without any strings attached. If you say, "I will give you $25,000 when you get married," it is not a gift. If there is a question of your mental competency at the time of the gift, the new ownership may be challenged. And, depending on the item being given, a gift is not complete until the ownership is legally changed, the item delivered, or the cheque is cashed.

Whom will you give what to? The choice is yours, with the condition that you cannot give away your family home, or property that belongs to your spouse, without his or her consent. You may want to give something to family members, friends, or charity. You may want to help your child or grandchild purchase a first home, start a business, pay for an education, or pay off some debts.

Depending on who receives the gift, you could continue to responsible for paying the tax on the future income earned on the asset. Table 4 summarizes the income attribution rules. The effect of the attribution rule on gifts is that even though you no longer own the asset, Revenue Canada might tax the income earned as if you still do! (After death, attribution rules no longer apply.)

TABLE 4

ATTRIBUTION RULES FOR GIFTS TO IMMEDIATE FAMILY

GIFT GIVEN TO	TYPE OF INCOME EARNED	PERSON RESPONSIBLE FOR TAX ON INCOME
spouse*	Interest	You
	Dividend	You
	Capital gains	You
trust for a spouse	Interest	You
	Dividend	You
	Capital gains	You
child under 18**	Interest	You
	Dividend	You
	Capital gains	Child
grandchild under 18**	Interest	You
	Dividend	You
	Capital gains	Grandchild

GIFT GIVEN TO	TYPE OF INCOME EARNED	PERSON RESPONSIBLE FOR TAX ON INCOME
child over 18	Interest	Child
	Dividend	Child
	Capital gains	Child
grandchild over 18	Interest	Grandchild
	Dividend	Grandchild
	Capital gains	Grandchild

includes common-law spouse
** *until child/grandchild turns 18*

GIVING AWAY PERSONAL POSSESSIONS

Some people mark personal items in their home with masking tape, such as on the bottom of the vase, to indicate the name of the person who is to receive it. Masking tape labels can and have been switched (sometimes by visiting young grandchildren who think that it's a great game!). To ensure that each item is given to the intended person, give it directly to the person while you are alive, include an itemized list in your will, or attach a letter to your will listing each item and who is to receive it. Some lawyers include a clause in the will stating that you are providing a letter or memorandum to assist your executor with distributing personal items. Then, if what you want to do with these items changes, you just have to redo the letter, not your entire will.

Family members often squabble over the assets, however small, that they would have liked to have had, or feel that they should have inherited. Granted, it may be hard to assess the true feelings of your offspring, but it may be helpful to future family relationships if you carefully note who is to get what. You might think, "If they are going to be so petty then they deserve what follows." But I think you owe it to future generations to anticipate their foibles under stress and lead the way.

Some people may be reluctant to accept a gift from you while you are alive, feeling it is morbid or premature. I believe that this is one way for people to get their lives in order and prepare to accept their own death. If you can, explain this to the recipient (and that you really want them to have the gift), and hope that they can accept it graciously.

GIVING TO YOUR ADULT CHILDREN

If you give your adult child cash, you may be able to reduce your future income taxes. You are not responsible for the taxes on the income earned on the cash—your child is.

EXAMPLE

Bob gives Sarah, his adult daughter $100,000. Assuming a 5% return, that $100,000 would earn $5,000 interest income annually. Since Bob was in the 50% tax bracket, he would save about $2,500 in tax every year from now on! If Sarah used the money to pay off her house, or as a down payment, no tax would be due. If she invested the money, she would have to pay tax on the income earned.

If the recipient is a young adult, giving cash so that he or she can make an RRSP contribution can provide years of tax-free growth on the investment.

If you give your adult child the cottage, mutual funds, stocks, or any asset other than cash, Revenue Canada assumes that you sold the asset at fair market value, even if no money changed hands. There could be a taxable capital gain that you will be required to report on your income tax return in that year.

Be very careful about giving just to reduce taxes or probate fees. I've seen families give so generously to their children that the spouse was left destitute. And a few families have put their cottages into their children's names, only to have one child later divorce or declare bankruptcy and lose the family cottage.

A LOAN VERSUS AN OUTRIGHT GIFT

Let's say you would like to give your adult child money now rather than later. Maybe you want to help him or her purchase a home but you are concerned about the stability of the marriage, or you just don't want to give the money outright. Consider lending the money and securing the loan by taking back a mortgage on his or her house. This strategy allows you to both help out your child and protect your estate. If the loan is used to buy a home, there is no income attribution.

If the loan was an attempt to split income and the money was used to make investments, the income can be attributed back to you.

GIFTS TO YOUNG CHILDREN

If you give money to a child or grandchild who is under 18, you are still responsible for paying income tax on any interest or dividends earned under the attribution rules. But if the gift given to a minor child or grandchild earns capital gains income, that income is *not* attributed back to you and the child is responsible for reporting the investment income at their (presumably) lower tax rate.

But any income earned on the income from the gift (sometimes called second-tier income) is not attributed to you, even if the gift originally earned interest or dividend income. This provides interesting tax planning opportunities.

EXAMPLE

You give your five-year-old granddaughter $10,000 to be invested in regular Canada Savings Bonds earning 6% in the first year. Under the attribution rules, you are responsible for the income tax due on the $600 of interest earned in year 1. But then the $600 interest is used to purchase an additional $600 in CSBs in your granddaughter's name. In year 2, you are responsible for the income tax earned on the original $10,000 of bonds, but your granddaughter is responsible for the tax on the interest earned on her $600 worth of CSBs. Assuming that the interest rate was still 6% and you were in the 50% tax bracket, this would save $18 dollars in income tax. Big deal, you say. But imagine how this adds up if you do it each year for 10 years or more.

Is it worth it? If you have the money available and have the discipline to move the income each year to the separate account for the child (and maintain a proper paper trail), you would lower your family's overall tax bill. If you are in a high tax bracket and dislike paying income taxes, this technique may be easier than earning an equivalent amount of after-tax income! After all, lowering the family tax bill is one way to preserve your estate for the next generation.

Q & A

Q. My father is now a resident of Florida. He wants to give my three children each $10,000 for their education. Does he have to pay income tax on the interest earned?

A. No. Attribution rules do not apply to gifts received from relatives who are not residents of Canada.

A Registered Education Savings Plan (RESP) can be a tax-effective way to give money to a child or grandchild to finance their post-secondary education. For any one beneficiary, the 1996 federal budget increased the maximum annual contribution from $1,500 to $2,000, and the lifetime limit from $31,500 to $42,000. While RESP contributions are not tax deductible, the earnings in the plan grow tax-free. If the child does not go on in their studies, the money contributed to the RESP can be withdrawn tax-free, but all the income earned is lost.

GIFTS TO CHARITIES AND CHARITABLE FOUNDATIONS

You can receive a non-refundable tax credit for gifts you make to a registered charity or charitable donation. (See Chapter 15 on gift planning.)

7
WHAT HAPPENS ON DEATH

After death, your will is located and read. If your executor, spouse, another family member, or lawyer knows the location of the will, it can usually be found quickly, but sometimes a will is not located for weeks because no one knew where it was. Occasionally, the lawyer will have the original and will invite the family in for a reading of the will, but mostly this is a scene from a Hollywood movie.

Q. My father died last week and we have the will in our possession. What should we do?

A. You may read the will and then ensure that the person named as the executor receives the original so they can carry out their responsibilities.

PROBATE

Your executor has to determine if your will must be probated—that is, if court approval must be obtained—to settle the estate and transfer the ownership of your assets. With a probated will, any third party can be certain that the executor has the legal authority to act on behalf of the estate. In other words, if a bank, say, takes instructions from the executor (where probate has been obtained) and it turns out that the executor's instructions were wrong, the bank cannot be held responsible. Some banks, trust companies, and other financial institutions have a standard practice of requiring probate so the executor can show that he or she has the proper authority.

Probating the will can generally not be avoided if any third party is involved who needs court approval to take instructions from the executor. These assets include

- assets at a financial institution that requires letters probate

- real estate in areas that require letters probate

- shares owned in a public company, or when shares in a private company are sold to someone outside the company.

Probate is also unavoidable if the executor needs to sue someone to settle the estate.

If your will needs to be probated, your executor will submit the original will, an inventory of the assets in the estate, and the completed application forms to the courts in the jurisdiction where you last lived. It may take an executor a few weeks to complete the application forms even if all the information is readily available. The application requires an itemized list of all the assets and property in the estate, including their market value at the time of your death. Your executor may want to obtain a lawyer's assistance with this application, though it does not legally require a lawyer.

If the will and all the correct papers are in good order, the courts will give their seal of approval and issue the letters probate or grant of probate document within a few weeks. In Ontario, letters probate are now formally called "the certificate of appointment of estate trustee with a will."

Q. *Does every will need to be probated?*

A. No. If the will and the estate are simple, there is no law requiring that the will be probated.

If the executor already has all of the assets in their possession, such as a spouse might, and does not need to deal with any third parties (such as financial institutions, new company owner, or creditors), letters probate will not be required. This might occur where the assets of the estate are mostly cash on hand and some personal effects.

For fairly small accounts, a financial institution may use discretion and waive the requirement for probate if it knows the family and the assets are being transferred within the family. But rules and policies do change.

In Quebec, probate is not required for a will that was prepared by a notary (under notary seal).

Not all wills are confirmed as completely valid by the courts. If the entire will is not accepted, the deceased is considered to have died intestate. Some wills contain provisions that are out of date or illegible, or it may not have been properly witnessed—all of which can be avoided. Sometimes the will itself is accepted as valid but is missing certain provisions, in which case those parts of the estate are generally handled as if the deceased died intestate. For example, a will might not deal with the residue of the estate or if a beneficiary named in the will has predeceased you. If so, the court will require that the intestate laws are followed for that portion of the estate.

The activities of the court are a matter of public record, including wills submitted for probate. The public, and the media, have access to the details in your will, including who is receiving what, and how much you owed and to whom. For those assets that flow through your will, this leaves your family, your business, and your beneficiaries no privacy. However, if your estate is unencumbered by mistresses, children born outside marriage, or questionable business dealings, this should cause you no concern.

To obtain information about a will being probated, contact the office of the provincial government in the area where the deceased lived. This office may be called the Probate, Surrogate, or the Wills and Estate Court.

After the will has been confirmed through probate, your executor can begin to transfer the assets in accordance with the terms of the will. It may take six months to two years or more before your beneficiaries receive the bulk of their inheritance. Some property can be transferred immediately, and other property cannot be transferred until all of the expenses of the estate have been paid.

Technically, your estate cannot be fully settled until the final income tax return has been filed and the estate receives a tax clearance certificate from Revenue Canada. The tax clearance certificate confirms that Revenue Canada is satisfied that the deceased's taxes have all been paid. Waiting for the tax clearance certificate protects the executor from any future income tax liability for the estate.

PROBATE FEES

Probate fees are paid out of the estate to the provincial court for issuing letters probate. The fees are based on the value of the assets that flow through the will. The higher the value, the higher the fee that is charged, although some provinces have a maximum fee (see Table 5). If just one asset in the estate requires the executor to apply for letters probate, then the value of *all* the assets flowing through the estate must be included in the calculation of the probate fees.

There is some debate as to whether probate fees are truly an administrative fee or just some form of death tax, especially in those provinces where there is no maximum. The amount of work required for the courts to probate a will (since most of the paperwork is completed by lawyers and not the government) is about the same whether an estate is worth $2 million or $200,000. But the cost to probate the will could be very different. Some people believe that the processing of probate should be a flat fee, since the "service" is essentially the same regardless of the value of the estate.

TABLE 5

Probate Fees Across Canada *		Maximum
Alberta	$25 for first $10,000 increasing to $6,000 for estates over $1,000,000	$6,000

PROBATE FEES ACROSS CANADA *		MAXIMUM
British Columbia	No fee for estates under $10,000; $140 (flat rate) for estates of $10,000 to $25,000; $6 on each $1,000 over $25,000	none
Manitoba	$20 for first $5,000 and $5 on each $1,000 over $5,000	none
New Brunswick	Up to $100 for the first $20,000 and $5 on each $1,000 over $20,000	none
Newfoundland	$50 for the first $1,000 and $4 on each $1,000 over $1,000	none
Northwest Territories	$8 for first $500 increasing to $15 for estate valued up to $1,000 and $3 on each $1,000 over $1,000	none
Nova Scotia	$75 for first $10,000 increasing to $800 for estate valued up to $200,000; $5 on each $1,000 over $200,000	none
Ontario	$5 on each $1,000 for first $50,000 and $15 on each $1,000 over $50,000	none
P.E.I.	$50 for first $10,000 increasing to $400 for estate of $400,000; $4 on each $1,000 over $400,000	none
Quebec	$45 for "English form" will; $0 for notarial wills	$45 none
Saskatchewan	$7 on each $1,000	none
Yukon	see British Columbia	

*as of April 1, 1996

Using Table 5, an estate valued at $1 million would face pro-
bate fees of $14,500 in Ontario. In New Brunswick, a $1 million
estate would face probate fees of $5,000. No wonder residents
of Ontario were so upset when the rates increased!

Q. *I live in Ontario and probate fees are lower in every other*
province. Can I have my will probated wherever I want?

A. Generally, your will is probated in the province where you
lived when you died. If you have property in more than one
province, your will may also have to be probated in that
other jurisdiction. (This is called re-sealing.) Additional probate fees are normally not charged.

In most provinces, probate fees are calculated on the market
value of your assets, not your net worth, and personal debts
(other than mortgages on personal real estate) are *not* deducted
before the fee is calculated. For example, if you have $300,000
of assets and property flowing through your estate and an unsecured line of credit for $100,000, probate fees would be based
on $300,000, not $200,000.

But that's not all. If probate is required to transfer assets to
your spouse on your death, it could be due again on those assets
when they are transferred through your spouse's will. Probate
fees are not waived when assets are transferred from one
spouse to the next. However, if the asset was held jointly with a
spouse, probate fees would be charged on that asset only when
the ownership passed through the will of the second spouse.

Probate fees cannot be deducted on the final income tax
return.

Q. *Probate fees were paid on my husband's property when it*
was transferred to me on his death. Are probate fees
payable again on my death?

A. Yes, if those assets are distributed through the instructions
in your will and any third party requires it.

STRATEGIES FOR REDUCING PROBATE FEES

Reducing probate fees should not be the primary focus of your estate plan. But why pay fees if you don't have to? Some strategies for reducing probate fees are relatively easy to implement and maintain, such as naming a beneficiary on your life insurance or pension plan. Other strategies may be inappropriate for your situation or could cost you or your estate more than the probate fees avoided. For example, you may not want to make your son a joint owner of your house, no matter how much it would save in probate fees! If you are planning to register property and assets jointly with married children, you could be exposing your assets to their marriage and creditor problems.

Before you decide on any technique to reduce probate fees, calculate the cost of implementing that technique as well as the potential savings. Costs could include re-registration of ownership, income taxes, legal fees, ongoing administration fees, land transfer tax (if the property has a mortgage), and maybe GST.

 Don't focus too much on reducing probate fees. You could end up doing something complex and expensive to save a relatively small amount in fees—and end up creating a tax problem and losing control of the asset.

A number of techniques and arrangements can be used to reduce probate fees, from simple to complex. Since probate fees are based on the value of the assets that flow through the will, the basic strategy to minimize these fees involves keeping as much out of the will as possible.

Let's look at how taking steps to transfer assets outside your estate can affect the value of your estate for probate purposes.

VALUE OF ESTATE FLOWING THROUGH THE WILL
BEFORE PLANNING FOR PROBATE

Marital home (registered in one name)	$200,000
Life insurance payable to estate	$100,000
Stocks and bonds in your name	$250,000
RRSP payable to estate	$ 30,000
Total value of estate for probate	$580,000

AFTER PLANNING FOR PROBATE

Marital home (owned jointly with spouse)	0
Life insurance payable to spouse	0
Stocks and bonds owned jointly with spouse	0
RRSP (spouse named as beneficiary)	0
Total value of estate for probate	0

If some probate fees will be payable, ensure that there will be enough cash on hand, or assets that could be sold, to pay them. Sometimes insurance is suggested as a way to provide enough funds to cover probate fees and final income taxes. But first determine if the fee is enough to warrant a life insurance policy.

> If just one financial institution requires probate, there may be an alternative to probating the will (and probate fees). The financial institution may accept a suitable security arrangement, such as a probate bond (like an insurance premium) or a letter of indemnity, to ensure it will not be held financially responsible if it follows the executor's directions.

DESIGNATED BENEFICIARIES

If you designate your estate as the beneficiary for your life insurance, pension plans, RRSP, and RRIFs, probate will be required because the distribution of those assets will flow through your will.

The simplest, cheapest, and most practical way to reduce or avoid probate fees is to name a beneficiary on your RRSP or RRIF with an insurance company and on your insurance policies so that the benefit does not form part of your estate and is not included in the calculation of the probate fee.

There is debate about whether naming beneficiaries on RRSPs and RRIFs held with banks and trust companies will avoid probate, since financial institutions can insist on probate to protect themselves before releasing funds. My survey of banks and trust companies indicated they were more concerned if the value of the RRSP or RRIF was over $30,000. Ask your financial institution about its policy. It might pay out the proceeds without probate if you post a bond or if it receives a letter from the estate's lawyer indemnifying the institution in the event the executor's instructions were incorrect. Regardless, if you name your spouse as the beneficiary on RRSPs and RRIFs, these assets can be passed to your spouse without income tax.

Keep your beneficiary designations up to date since these assets are distributed according to the last beneficiary on record. If your spouse is your beneficiary, consider adding an alternate beneficiary to cover the possibility that you both die at the same time.

JOINT OWNERSHIP OF ASSETS

Registering the ownership of assets, such as the family home, shares, bonds, or mutual funds as joint tenants, or joint tenants with rights of survivorship, is another technique used to reduce probate fees. On financial statements, you may see the term "JTWROS" after both your names.

When property is registered as joint tenants with rights of survivorship, the deceased's interest in the asset is automatically passed to the surviving owner. This transfer is not handled by the will; it is covered by other laws. The assets stay out of the estate and therefore are not included in the calculation of probate fees. For example, let's assume that you and your spouse are the joint owners of a bank account registered with rights of survivorship. When one spouse dies, the surviving spouse is automatically entitled to all the money in the account. No probate is needed to transfer ownership.

However, an asset registered as tenancy *in common* is treated differently. It does not automatically transfer to the other registered owner. On death it transfers according to the instructions in the deceased's will.

It often makes good sense for spouses or common-law spouses to own assets jointly, but it can be full of problems if it is with anyone else. I don't recommend joint ownership just to avoid probate fees. It also has to make good common sense.

Although it is relatively easy to change the registered ownership of assets, you should consider the disadvantages of joint ownership.

- You lose exclusive control of the asset.

- If the other person named files for bankruptcy, creditors could seize the asset.

- If the asset is real estate, you require the consent of the joint owner to sell it.

- If the asset is a bank account, the joint owner could withdraw funds without your consent (such as a spouse leaving the marriage).

- If property is classified as a matrimonial home (house or cottage), the property could be affected as part of a divorce settlement.

- Revenue Canada will consider that you "sold" a portion of the asset to that individual at fair market value (unless it was to a spouse). If there was profit from the "sale," even if it was only on paper, income taxes could be due.

- If the joint registration is done in name only (solely to avoid probate fees) and is not a true transfer of ownership and the rights of ownership, technically it may not be enough to keep the asset out of the probate fee calculation.

As for income tax, the individual who contributed the money to acquire the asset is responsible for the tax on any income, subject to the attribution rules, and on any profits at the time the property was transferred (unless it was to a spouse).

Q. *I have a portfolio of mutual funds and stocks that are registered in only my name. To reduce probate fees, I want to register these investments jointly with my adult son. Will there be any costs involved?*

A. Probably. Revenue Canada will consider there to have been a sale, or a "deemed disposition," of the assets in your portfolio. If there is a capital gain (profit) from "selling" 50% of the portfolio to your son, you are responsible for the income tax on that gain. In addition, there may be commission or transfer fees to change the account registration and/or the re-registration of the certificates.

Two things to keep in mind: RRSPs and RRIFs cannot be owned jointly. And in Quebec, there is no joint tenancy with automatic right of survivorship.

Real Estate

Real estate that is registered in joint tenancy does not pass through a will and does not require probating. Legally, joint tenancy provides the surviving owner with the deceased's share of the property.

Q & A

Q. *Should I register my house jointly with my daughter? My husband died last year.*

A. That depends. You would be giving up the ability to completely control the house. If you want to sell the house, you will need your daughter's written consent. If your daughter is married and is living in the house with her husband and her marriage breaks up, it gets even more complex. If she is registered as a joint owner of "your" house, the house could be considered the matrimonial home (which has special status depending on provincial family law). To avoid this situation, it is sometimes suggested that the spouse-in-law sign a single-purpose marriage contract (even if they've already been married for a number of years) agreeing not to claim any interest in the home. Although good in theory, this may not be a practical step unless all parties are in agreement and understand the legal, personal, and financial implications. After considering the disadvantages of joint ownership, you may decide it is inappropriate to add another name to the ownership even if it means probate fees will be paid.

If there is a mortgage on the property, the lender generally must approve the addition of the second owner. If the name being added is your spouse, this is usually a formality. There may be legal costs to re-register the ownership.

> If you originally registered your home or cottage in your spouse's name to protect the house from any professional liability or, because under old laws each spouse used to be able to have a principal residence, review your situation and determine whether it still makes sense to keep the house in one name only. A house worth $500,000 registered jointly could save your estate up to $7,000 in probate fees in Ontario, less in other provinces.

If you are asked to be the second name on, say, your mother's house, consider if this strategy is in your best interests.

• If you have your own principal residence, *you* may have to pay income tax on any profits on your share when your mother's property is eventually sold—which could be greater than the probate fees potentially saved.

• If you do not have your own home and live in your mother's house, you could lose the ability to participate in some of the government programs for first-time home buyers, such as the RRSP loan program, because technically you would be an owner.

Other Assets

To change the registration on investment accounts, you would request the issuer to add the second name with a right of survivorship. For guaranteed investment certificates, the ownership normally can be changed at renewal. For mutual funds or stocks, the investments may need to be sold and repurchased under the new names which may trigger taxable capital gains. Consult with your advisor before proceeding. On money market and bank accounts, ownership can be changed without triggering capital gains.

EXAMPLE

Steve had $500,000 in money market mutual funds. As part of his estate planning, he re-registered these jointly with his spouse, Sheila, for two reasons:

1) to ensure that Sheila would have access to "their" money if he died suddenly, and

2) to reduce probate fees.

No fees were charged to re-register the ownership of these funds, and since there was no "profit" no taxes were triggered. Although Steve is still responsible for reporting the annual income from these funds, this paperwork will save his estate about $7,500 in probate fees (Ontario) and give Sheila quicker access to the money.

Canada Savings Bonds can be registered jointly when purchased or when existing bonds mature. If the bonds are registered jointly with rights of survivorship, the Bank of Canada will re-register them in the name of the surviving owner after proof of death has been provided. The Bank of Canada does not require probate for Canada Savings Bonds valued under $20,000.

GIFTS

Giving away cash or other assets during your lifetime will reduce probate fees. The basic premise of this technique is simple. If you don't own the asset at the time of your death, it does not form part of your estate. I never recommend giving assets away *just* to save probate fees or future income taxes. You want to ensure that it fits your personal situation and that you have taken care of your future needs and those of your spouse.

Watch out, though. Giving non-cash assets may be considered a "sale" in the eyes of Revenue Canada and fall under the attribution rules. You do not have to receive a cash payment for Revenue Canada to consider there to be a profit. Let's say you want to give your adult daughter your Bank of Nova Scotia shares that cost you $1,000 and are now worth $12,000. According to Revenue Canada, if the value of the property when the gift is made is greater than the value of the property when you acquired it, there is a profit. In this example, income tax would be due on $11,000 of profit when the gift was made. If you gave your daughter $12,000 cash, you would not have the tax bill (unless you sold the shares to raise the cash).

You can transfer some or all of your assets to your beneficiaries before your death, especially when death may occur soon. While this may be difficult to discuss, there could be some practical benefits. It could make the estate simpler to administer and save some probate fees.

It is also possible to give a gift on your death bed, using the enduring power of attorney. This type of gift is known as *donatio mortis causa* and could reduce probate fees by keeping the value of the gift outside your estate.

MULTIPLE WILLS

Multiple wills are one of the newer methods lawyers use to reduce probate fees. There are two variations on the use of multiple wills.

1) For different assets in one province: Two wills are prepared, one to deal with the assets that will *not* require probate and one for those assets that *will* require probate (such as shares in a family business). After death, probate fees would be calculated only on the assets flowing through the second will. These wills need to be tested in court before we can be sure of their effectiveness. But even if this strategy did not stand up in court, you would end up paying probate on the combined amount (which is what would have happened without the second will).

2) For assets in different provinces: This strategy assumes that probate fees can be saved if some of your assets are probated in a province with lower probate fees. You prepare two wills, one to deal with the assets in the province where you live and a second for those assets held in a province with a lower probate schedule. Again, you have to look at the costs involved to set up this strategy, the potential savings in probate fees, and whether it makes good personal and business sense. And there is nothing to prevent the other provinces from following Ontario's example and raising probate fees to try to reduce government debt.

EXAMPLE

Joan has a private corporation worth $1.5 million located in Ontario. She is considering moving this corporation to Alberta to reduce the cost of probate. Since the maximum fee in Alberta is $6,000, this would save about $16,000 in probate fees.

Multiple wills should be drawn up only with the advice of a lawyer. You need to ensure that the second will does not revoke the first will.

TRUSTS

Probate fees are charged each time the ownership of assets is transferred through a will. For example, if you leave your $100,000 stock portfolio to your spouse in your will, probate fees will be charged on your stocks. On your spouse's death, when the stock portfolio is transferred to your children, probate fees will be charged a second time on those assets. To avoid paying probate a second time, the stock portfolio might be held in a spousal testamentary trust set up in your will, if it fits in with the overall plan. Then, on the death of your spouse, the stocks would be distributed to your children according to the instructions of the trust agreement rather than your spouse's will.

Some wills contain a clause that is sometimes referred to as a joint disaster clause or a 30-day survival clause. The clause may say something like, if your spouse does not outlive you for more than 30 days, other beneficiaries (say, your children) will receive your spouse's inheritance. If triggered, this clause has the effect of saving probate fees because, rather than your assets going to your spouse and then to your children, they go directly to your children.

Another method sometimes used to reduce probate fees is to transfer assets to a living trust while you are alive. These assets would not require probate because technically they are not your property at the time of death. These assets would be transferred to your beneficiaries according to the instructions in the trust agreement, rather than through your will. To make this technique worth the bother, the total amount of the probate fees saved should be significant enough to offset the costs of setting up the trust and the ongoing trust expenses. (See Chapter 13 for a discussion of trusts.)

CONVERTING PERSONAL DEBT TO SECURED OR CORPORATE DEBT

If you have no debts, or don't intend to have any future debts, or if your only debt is a personal mortgage, this section does not apply to you.

Except for a personal mortgage, personal debts *cannot* be deducted from the value of your assets before probate fees are calculated. So if, at the time of your death, you have assets valued at $100,000 and personal liabilities (such as credit cards or an unsecured line of credit) of $40,000, probate fees would be calculated on the assets valued at $100,000, not on $60,000. But debts held in a personal corporation or holding company can be deducted before probate fees are calculated.

If you live in a province that has no limit on probate fees and you have a fair-sized unsecured line of credit, you might consider replacing the unsecured line of credit with a personal mortgage or just paying it off. Based on the probate fee schedule in your province, you can calculate the reduction in probate fees and the overall savings after the legal fees are paid to register the mortgage (see Table 5).

EXAMPLE

Personal debts	$400,000	
Personal assets		$ 1,050,000
Value of corporation		$ 800,000
Total estate for probate		$ 1,850,000

Probate fees payable (using Ontario's schedule):

0.5% on first $50,000 =	$ 250
1.5% on $1,800,000 =	$ 27,500
Total probate fees	$ 27,750

If you have a corporation or a holding company and personal debt, you may want to rearrange your affairs so that the corporation holds the debt, or hold the debt as a personal mortgage.

Personal assets		$1,050,000
Assets of corporation	$ 800,000	
Corporate debt	−$ 400,000	
Net value of corporation		$ 400,000
Total estate for probate		$1,450,000
Probate fees payable:		
0.5% on first $50,000 =		$ 250
1.5% on $1,400,000 =		$ 21,000
Total probate fees		$ 21,250

To determine whether it makes sense as part of your overall business objectives and from the cost-benefit side, calculate the costs of setting up the corporation (if it does not already exist), continuing administration fees, and refinancing, as well as the cost of probate in your province.

SUMMARY

This chapter has described some of the strategies that have been used to reduce probate fees. If you live in a province with high probate fees, you might be interested in implementing strategies to save a few dollars. But don't let the tail (in this case, probate fees) wag the dog!

8
FINANCIAL
POWERS OF ATTORNEY

"My mother was smart. She signed a power of attorney before she entered the hospital, so that I was able to pay her bills and renegotiate her rent. I don't know how our family would have managed without that power of attorney. I've seen how important the document can be, so I prepared the documents so that my sons can help me out if it ever becomes necessary." M.

So far, we have been looking at estate planning in terms of planning your affairs for the transfer of assets to your beneficiaries. However, estate planning is more than that. What if you are seriously hurt in a car accident and lying in a coma in the hospital? Or mentally incapacitated by a stroke? Or out of the country for an extended time? Or are dealing with a severely debilitating condition? Your mortgage and other bills will still have to be paid.

Situations like these can arise at any time, not just with advancing years, and they are *not* covered by your will. A power of attorney should be considered as part of estate planning. You don't have to have oodles of assets or be elderly for it to be essential. Things happen.

You may believe, like many people, that if you become incapacitated through an accident or illness, your spouse or child can automatically look after your financial affairs, including paying your bills and managing your assets. This is not true. Without a signed power of attorney naming them, your immediate family has no legal right to control your finances—at least, not without obtaining court approval.

And if you and your spouse jointly own your home, family law or matrimonial property law may require the signature of both spouses for transactions involving the matrimonial home, even if only one spouse is named on the title of the property. If you are declared mentally incompetent and did not name a power of attorney, your spouse will have to obtain court approval to sell or mortgage the home.

Q & A

Q. I've signed a power of attorney at my bank. Do I need another one?

A. The power of attorney at the bank covers only specific assets at that bank. If you have other assets, the bank power of attorney form is not enough! If the attorney you've appointed at the bank is not the same person you've appointed as your general power of attorney, you might want to document that in your general power of attorney to prevent confusion.

The financial power of attorney is a separate document from a will and is sometimes referred to as a power of attorney for personal property, a power of attorney for financial decisions, representative, or just a power of attorney. In Quebec, the document is called a mandate. The authority given the attorney is valid only while you are alive—it stops on your death. After death your will comes into effect, appointing an executor to look after your estate. People often prepare a power of attorney document when they write or update their will. The person named as the attorney and executor may be the same, but they get their authority from different documents.

THE POWER OF ATTORNEY DOCUMENT

A power of attorney is a "pre-estate" document that grants the person or persons named the right to manage your financial affairs on your behalf while you are alive.

Preparing a power of attorney in advance allows you to choose who will look after things for you if you are temporarily or permanently unable to. If you do not formally appoint someone to act on your behalf to protect your interests, a government office—the Office of the Public Guardian and Trustee—will step in to look after your affairs and protect your rights.

In some cases, the public trustee will manage your assets and property if you are incapable of managing your own affairs and have not signed a power of attorney. But the public trustee may well make decisions that are different from those your family members or friends might make. The decisions may or may not be satisfactory to the family but the laws are designed to protect your interests. The public trustee is permitted to take possession of your bank accounts, bonds, and all other assets, without consulting your family—regardless of how ethical and supportive your family is.

It is a misconception that the government is waiting to take over whenever possible. One Office of the Public Guardian and Trustee describes itself as the "decision-maker of the last resort." In the event that you become mentally incapacitated and do not have a power of attorney in place, a family member can apply to the public trustee to be appointed as your attorney or representative. To protect its own liability, the public trustee assesses all applications and may require even close family members to post a bond or security and file a management plan and monitor their decisions. These are all things that we don't normally want our spouses or other relatives to have to do under difficult circumstances. The best thing to do is to appoint a power of attorney for yourself in advance to save your family the added stress.

Q. Does my power of attorney need to be a lawyer?

A. No. The "attorney" is just the term for the person you name. Your "attorney" could be a spouse, relative, or trusted friend. You are not required to have a power of attorney. If necessary, the government will step in until someone can be appointed.

Unless restrictions are specified, a power of attorney document authorizes the "attorney" to act on your behalf for any financial act that you would legally be able to do, except prepare or change your will. The extent of the powers given to an attorney may be:

- *general,* giving the power to do all financial acts, such as paying your bills, arranging a mortgage, selling your investments, or withdrawing money from your bank, or

- *limited* to specific transactions, such as selling your house while you are out of the country, performing banking transactions, or handling your Canada Pension Plan cheques for you because you find it difficult to get out.

Unless your power of attorney document contains the correct language, it will be revoked by mental incapacity. To have the power of attorney continue to be valid even if you are later declared incompetent (which is the only reason many people prepare a power of attorney), it must contain the correct wording so that it *endures* or *continues* even if you become mentally incompetent. ("Enduring" is just the old legal word for continuing.) Wording similar to "survives my subsequent incapacity" under your province's act is necessary to prevent your power of attorney from being cancelled if you become mentally incompetent. In Quebec, the document must state that it "is in contemplation of incapacity."

Q. Who decides if I am not capable of managing my own affairs?

A. Sometimes the decision is easy, such as if you are in a coma after a car accident. If you become a resident of a psychiatric facility, your physician might decide. There is a review process if someone's capacity is in question. But as a general rule, you are assumed to be capable unless there is good reason to believe you are not.

If You Live in Ontario

For Ontario residents, the Office of the Public Trustee has information kits containing a guidebook and sample power of attorney forms. They can be obtained by calling the Office of the Public Trustee at (416) 314-2800 or at your local MPP's office.

In Ontario, if there is no power of attorney in place, the *Substitute Decisions Act* allows a person to apply to the Office of the Public Trustee to become the guardian of a mentally incapacitated person's property without going to court. This guardian must file a management plan for the assets and may be required to provide a bond (like a premium for an insurance policy), or security for the assets. The court can waive the requirement, especially when the guardian is a family member and the assets are family assets. My feeling is that I would not like this decision made at the discretion of a court official. As we become a more litigious society, I believe that the courts will be less prepared to waive this type of coverage making it even more important to have the proper documents in place.

If You Live in British Columbia

British Columbia is expected to proclaim the *B.C. Representation Act* (similar to Ontario's *Substitute Decisions Act*) late in 1996. This law allows adults in B.C. to appoint a representative to make financial decisions using a representative agreement with either standard or enhanced provisions. The representative must act according to the adult's beliefs and values, if known. To protect the adult assigning the representative agreement from potential abuses, the adult may appoint a monitor to watch over the decisions of the representative. The appointment of a monitor may be waived.

SELECTING YOUR POWER OF ATTORNEY

The person named as your attorney must be able to make good financial decisions on your behalf. He or she has the following responsibilities:

- to act in your best interest (not their own) and in good faith
- to avoid conflicts of interest
- to exercise good judgement on your behalf
- to maintain records
- to consult with you wherever possible.

The person should be someone you trust unconditionally who also has the ability to do the job. Look at how they manage their own financial affairs. Is that how you want your affairs handled? Typically, people name their spouse, a trusted family member, or a close friend. If you choose not to name your spouse, or name someone to act jointly with your spouse, be sure to discuss with your spouse whom you have named and why. Your spouse could become extremely frustrated with the day-to-day management of the family's financial affairs if he or she is required to report to a third person. Your lawyer may ask you if you can really trust that person. You'll have to use your best judgement.

Trust companies and lawyers can also be appointed as a power of attorney (or a backup) where no one is able or willing to be appointed.

We've talked about naming backup executors and backup guardians, and I also recommend that you name an alternate attorney, in case the first is unable or unwilling to act when required. Select you backup with the same care you made for your main choice.

Q. *My father has just died after a long illness. My brother was his attorney at the bank. We think that there should be more money left, but it seems to be all gone. What can we do?*

A. Unfortunately, mismanagement or abuses by the attorney may not be discovered until after death. If you can prove fraud, you could consider laying charges.

Your attorney is not required to make exactly the same decisions that you might have made if you were able. However, you can assist your attorney by providing written instructions in advance stating how you would like your assets or property to be handled should you become incapacitated, especially if there may be major decisions to be made. (It's one thing to lose your mental abilities forever; it's another thing to be in a coma for six months and wake up to find that decisions have been made that you have to live with.) You may also give your attorney the right to see your will so that he or she can manage your affairs in a way that reflects your overall intentions. Although such written instructions do provide some guidance, they are not legally binding on your attorney.

THE POWERS OF THE ATTORNEY

The powers should not be assigned lightly since a full power of attorney gives that person the legal authority to do anything that you can do, including withdrawing money from your bank account, buying or selling real estate, making gifts to charity, loaning money, and transferring securities. Because the power of attorney is such a powerful document, it is open to abuse. Police have seen many abuses of powers of attorney, by family members, as well as business associates. To reduce the risk of fraud, exploitation, and mismanagement, choose the person carefully and consider building some limitations into the powers of attorney.

A power of attorney can be given powers as extensive or as limited as you see fit. Limitations and safeguards place restrictions on your attorney but they may keep your attorney from acting quickly when necessary. For example, if you give instructions that the power of attorney cannot be used unless you are declared mentally incompetent, your attorney will need to have independent doctors document that fact. But you may want your attorney to be able to act for you when you are physically unable, but still mentally competent. Without proper legal advice it's an easy mistake to make.

The following list shows some limitations and safeguards that people have incorporated into their powers of attorney to reduce abuses. This is not a list of recommended limitations. Review the list and consider whether any of these safeguards are required for your situation.

- Have a third party, such as your lawyer, hold the power of attorney documents with written instructions as to when the forms should be released to the named power of attorney.

- Place limits on the powers that the attorney has, by specifying what it can and cannot be used for, and under what conditions.

- Select more than one person to act jointly as co-attorneys so that one person does not have all the control or the responsibility. "Jointly" means they must act together; "jointly and severally" means they can act together or separately. But consider if this is practical. If your two daughters live a thousand miles apart, there will be some delay when their signatures are required.

- Document that the power of attorney cannot be used unless you are declared mentally incompetent. Some lawyers do not recommend that you do this because it can make it difficult to confirm when your attorney has the legal authority to act, and it restricts your attorney from acting for you when the problem is not related to mental competency. Your financial institution may want to see the medical certificate declaring that you are mentally incompetent, as well as the power of attorney document.

PREPARING A POWER OF ATTORNEY

To prepare a power of attorney, you must have attained the age of majority in your province and be mentally competent. In some provinces, do-it-yourself kits are available. But be forewarned. Some lawyers have suggested that these kits leave room for people to make errors.

It currently costs less than $100 to prepare a power of attorney through a lawyer, although in some provinces it is not required that you see a lawyer to prepare the document. Nevertheless, wherever you are, I recommend that you consult with a lawyer. If the power of attorney needs to be used, I would want you to be sure that it would be acceptable to your financial institutions.

The statements required in the power of attorney document vary from province to province. Your lawyer will be able to ensure that your power of attorney meets all of your province's requirements. For example, in Alberta, an enduring power of attorney requires a lawyer to certify that you understood the power of the document and were mentally competent at the time. In Manitoba, if you want your attorney to be able to deal with the family home, you must specifically state that you are giving your attorney powers under the *Homestead Act*. If preparing a new enduring power of attorney in Ontario, the document should make reference to the *Mental Health Act*.

Power of attorney documents must be properly witnessed to reduce the potential for abuse. In Ontario, all power of attorney documents signed since 1995 require two witnesses who do not have certain relationships with you.

If you have property in other provinces or states, you should also determine if you require an attorney document in those locations.

Q. *My mother is 85 and refuses to give my brother and me a power of attorney. What can we do?*

A. Nothing. It is her right not to prepare a power of attorney. However, someone must manage her financial affairs if she is unable to. Many people prefer to choose that someone rather than leaving the decisions to a government agency. Your mother may feel that she does not trust you enough, or feel that an independent body such as the public trustee is appropriate for her situation. No one is required to sign a power of attorney. It should be done only if a person feels it is in their best interests, for both the short and long term.

REVIEWING A POWER OF ATTORNEY

A power of attorney document does not expire. Periodically, you should review this document, perhaps when you review your will, to ensure that it still meets your requirements and the person named is still willing to act on your behalf.

REVOKING A POWER OF ATTORNEY

A power of attorney document is revoked

• by your death. After death, your executor is given the authority to manage your affairs.

- by mental incapacity, unless the power of attorney document contains the correct legal wording so that it will survive a mental incapacity

- by the death of the person named as the attorney, unless you have named a backup.

- by delivering a letter to the person named as the attorney stating that the power of attorney has been revoked, as long as you are mentally able.

    You should also notify all the people that the attorney may have dealt with on your behalf and inform them that the power of attorney has been revoked. This might include your bank, your financial advisor, and your mortgage company. It is also recommended that you obtain the original power of attorney document.

COMPENSATING A POWER OF ATTORNEY

The person acting as your attorney may be entitled to be reimbursed for all expenses related to looking after your affairs, such as postage, and mileage to go to your bank. In some provinces, your attorney is legally entitled to compensation according to a set fee scale. When a spouse acts as the attorney, he or she does not normally request compensation.

Q. Should I set my assets up in a trust rather than use a power of attorney?

A. If your financial situation is particularly complex, a trust might be more appropriate than a power of attorney document, since it would more formally specify what is to be done with your assets. However, for most people, a power of attorney document will protect their interests in the event of mental incompetency.

SUMMARY

Everyone over 18 who owns assets and property should have a financial power of attorney if they know an appropriate individual they can appoint. Preparing a power of attorney ensures that a person of your choice—and not some official in a government office—will make decisions on your behalf. With careful planning, you have more options to set up your affairs. You decide who decides.

9

DEATH AND TAXES

"Nothing can be said to be certain, except death and taxes."
Ben Franklin

Death taxes, inheritance taxes, succession duties, estate taxes—they all have more or less the same meaning to Canadians. And they're nothing new. When George Gooderham, president of the Bank of Toronto and son of the founder of the distilling firm Gooderham and Worts, died in 1905, the succession duties on his estate were more than enough to eliminate the entire debt of the province of Ontario!

All estate taxes were eliminated in the early 1970s. Even so, your government is waiting for you to die so it can collect income tax on the undeclared profits on assets and property (unless they are left to your spouse). Revenue Canada wants us to pay up on death!

How long do you think the government can ignore the estimated $1 trillion that is expected to pass from one generation to the next? In the United States, estate taxes are calculated on the total wealth a person has at the time of death, and there has been speculation that the U.S. style of estate taxes is coming here. In 1993, the Ontario Fair Tax Commission recommended reintroducing estate taxes at the federal level. (After all, which province would want to be the first to bring in estate taxes?) Just imagine how much tax could be collected from even a portion of that $1 trillion. It's little wonder our governments consider reintroducing some form of estate tax from time to time.

Canada has special rules for the final tax return of a deceased person (called the terminal return). One of the responsibilities of the executor is to file the final income tax return for all income earned in that year, up to the date of death. In addition, assets the deceased owned are deemed to have been sold at death, even if no sale took place, and tax must be paid on the capital gains (profits) unless they were left to the spouse. Although this is not called a death tax, Revenue Canada wants to collect undeclared capital gains before the asset is transferred to a beneficiary.

Q. *How much income tax will need to be paid on the final tax return?*

A. That depends on the assets owned at the time of death, the profit on those assets, who the beneficiaries are, and the deceased's income for that final year. If a substantial profit in those assets is still untaxed, the deemed disposition rule could result in a hefty tax bill and more than half of the value of RRSPs or RRIFs could be taxed away—if not left to your spouse.

At the back of this book are forms that you can use to estimate your assets and liabilities at death. There are two versions of these forms: one to use if you have a spouse and one to use if you do not. Even if you are married, I recommend that you complete both worksheets, using the second worksheet to do some advance planning for when the assets will pass to the next generation.

Considering the income tax rules as part of your estate planning can help to reduce or even eliminate the taxes due—unless you really want the government to be one of your beneficiaries. If you can plan to minimize the immediate effect of the deemed disposition rule, more of your estate will be left intact for your beneficiaries.

PRINCIPAL RESIDENCE

Your principal residence—that is, your home—is exempt from capital gains and can be left to any beneficiary without attracting any tax related to capital gains. In most provinces, spouses have a protected interest in the matrimonial home and it cannot be gifted or sold out from under them (see Chapter 11).

If the market value of a home increases while it is part of your estate (from the date of death but before it is transferred or sold), this portion of the profit is taxable to the estate.

SPOUSAL TRANSFERS

The simplest way to defer the taxes on death is to name your spouse as the beneficiary on RRSPs or RRIFs *and* to leave him or her all other assets. Assets left to your spouse, outright or through a trust, receive favourable tax treatment: non-registered assets can be transferred at the deceased's original cost, called a rollover, and the tax on any capital gains is deferred until your spouse dies.

Of course, on the death of your spouse, his or her executor must include any capital gains on those assets on the final tax return *as* if they had been sold on the date of death. Remember, tax bills don't go away. Sometimes they are just deferred until another day. (Also see "Registered Plans" later in this chapter.)

As part of longer-range tax planning and to keep more for the next generation, it is sometimes advantageous to declare some or all of the profits on the final tax return and elect *not* to roll over all the assets to the spouse. For example, if the deceased's income is low in the year of death, it may make sense to transfer some or all the assets to the spouse at a higher cost and pay the tax on the final return—if it won't result in a huge tax bill. In other cases, if the deceased had unused capital losses at death, the executor might use them to offset the other income on the final tax return, or in the previous year.

EXAMPLE

At death, Paul has taxable capital gains of $300,000 and capital losses totalling $50,000. His executor elects to roll over $250,000 of the estate to Paul's wife, Linda, tax-free and to declare $50,000 of the capital gains to offset the capital loss. The net result on the final tax return is the same as if the executor had rolled over the entire $300,000.

The real benefit of this technique comes when Linda dies two months later; the value of the assets has not changed. Linda's final tax return has no rollover option (it would if she had quickly remarried), so $250,000 of capital gains must be included, but not the other $50,000 that had been declared previously.

The net tax saving to the next generation by offsetting the gains with losses is $25,000 (assuming a 50% tax bracket).

If your spouse decides to sell any of these assets after they have been rolled over, he or she would pay tax on the profits on the current year's income tax return.

ADDITIONAL CONTRIBUTIONS
TO A SPOUSAL RRSP AFTER DEATH

If the deceased had unused RRSP contribution room and is survived by a spouse or a common-law spouse who is under 72 (lowered to 70 by 1997), the executor or personal representative can contribute to a spousal RRSP and create an additional deduction for the final income tax return. The contribution must be made in the year of death, or up to 60 days after that year end.

EXAMPLE

John died on November 30, 1995, and was survived by his wife. At the time of death, he had $10,000 unused RRSP contribution room. His executor elected to contribute $10,000 to a spousal RRSP on February 1, 1996. Since John was in the top marginal tax rate, this saved about $5,000 in taxes on his final income tax return.

If your spouse is not your sole beneficiary under your will, other family members may be expecting to share the residue. But a spousal RRSP contribution would reduce the amount available to the other beneficiaries and they may perceive this as unfair to them. To defuse a potential conflict, you could give your executor the discretion to make this decision in your will.

ASSETS NOT LEFT TO A SPOUSE

Revenue Canada considers that assets and property you owned (and did not leave to your spouse) were sold at fair market value at the time of death, even though no actual sale took place. This is called a deemed disposition. If assets are deemed to have been sold at a profit, the capital gain could mean a substantial tax bill on your final return.

Some people believe that everything they own has to be sold on death, but this is not true. Assets and property do not have to be *actually* sold unless it is necessary to raise cash to pay taxes or other liabilities.

Note that a principal residence is exempt from capital gains. Capital gains did not exist in Canada before 1972, so taxable profits are based on the increase in value from December 31, 1971 (called valuation day or V-day), or the day the asset was acquired, if later. If the asset is real estate but not a principal residence, the rules are more complicated.

RRSPs or RRIFs not left to a spouse are considered to have been cashed in and are taxed.

TAX IMPLICATIONS
WHEN NAMING BENEFICIARIES

It is important to consider how the tax rules work when you are naming beneficiaries in your will. Let's assume your intention is to leave some assets to your spouse and some assets to other family members. If you leave the assets with the capital gains to your spouse and the assets with little or no capital gains to the others, little or no tax will be immediately due on death. This in itself is an important tax planning tool, but it must not be considered in isolation from your other estate planning objectives.

EXAMPLE

You have a portfolio of mutual funds that cost $25,000 in 1980. These investments have done well and have a current market value of $125,000. As of February 22, 1994, you had used up all of your capital gains exemption on other assets. You are reviewing your estate plan and are considering leaving this portfolio to either your spouse or your brother. Look at the difference in the tax treatment.

MUTUAL FUND PORTFOLIO LEFT TO	SPOUSE	BROTHER
Value of deemed disposition	$25,000	$125,000
Adjusted cost base	$25,000	$ 25,000
Resulting capital gain on death	0	$100,000
Taxable capital gain (75%) on final return	0	$75,000
Taxes due on final return (assuming 50% tax rate)	0	$37,500

Left to your brother, about $37,500 in tax would be due from the profits on these investments, not including surtaxes. Left to your spouse, the tax on this portfolio could be deferred until the death of your spouse (unless your spouse sold them earlier).

THE $100,000 CAPITAL GAINS EXEMPTION

Since 1994, it has no longer been possible to reduce taxes by claiming capital gains under the $100,000 capital gains exemption. Now, 75% of *all* capital gains (net of capital losses) must be reported as taxable income, creating a higher tax liability and a bigger problem for people who wish to preserve assets or the value of their estate. It would be a shame if your family had to sell a business or cottage that you wanted to keep in the family just to pay your final tax bill. A forced sale is never desirable, and is even worse if the market value is down.

Over the years, the taxable amount of capital gains has increased and the capital gains exemption has decreased. In 1987, the first $100,000 of capital gains was exempt from tax and only 50% of the capital gains over $100,000 was taxed. In 1996, 75% of all capital gains were taxable. For example, if James died in 1987, had no spouse, and had property with a capital gain of $600,000, the tax bill on his final tax return would have been about $125,000. But if James had died in early 1996, with a capital gain of $600,000, the tax bill would be about $225,000. That's a significantly different tax bill!

T I P

Late elections for the $100,000 capital gains exemption can be filed by taxpayers until April 30, 1997, with a penalty. The penalty is 1/3 of 1% of the amount of the taxable capital gains elected, multiplied by the number of months that the election is late. As well, there is a late filing penalty. The penalty may be small change compared with the hundreds or thousands of dollars you could save in income tax.

In my opinion, the elimination of the $100,000 capital gains exemption was a form of estate tax—for some Canadians, death was the only time they ever claimed any of the capital gains exemption.

The $500,000 capital gains exemption still exists for qualified small business corporations and qualified farm property.

INCOME TAXES DUE FROM CAPITAL GAINS

To estimate just how much income tax would be due from capital gains on your final tax return, you need to take a snapshot of your current situation. Use the "Personal Inventory" forms at the back of this book. List all your assets not left to your spouse, their cost base for Revenue Canada purposes, and their current market value. Then calculate the undeclared profits on each asset since 1972 by subtracting the cost from the market value and unused capital losses. What's 40% of that? That's an estimate of the income taxes that would be due from the capital gains on your assets and property at the time of death. For a more exact figure, see your advisor. Since the value of your assets will change over time, the tax estimate should be recalculated periodically.

EXAMPLE

In 1973, Georges bought 1,000 shares at $10 each. When Georges died, these shares were worth $50 each and were left to his daughter in his will. The income taxes due on these shares would be calculated as follows:

Fair market value of shares at time of death	$50,000
Cost	$10,000
Capital gain (profit)	$40,000
75% of capital gain (taxable portion)	$30,000
Taxes payable (assuming 50% tax rate)	$15,000

The income tax due is the same as if Georges had sold the shares through his broker while he was alive.

If you sell an asset that has significant capital gains while you are alive, you may end up paying alternate minimum tax. Alternate minimum tax is a tax calculation designed to ensure that people with large amounts of preferential tax deductions, such as capital gains, pay at least a minimum amount of tax on the profit. If the tax based on the alternate minimum tax calculation is greater than the tax calculated on the regular tax return, the greater amount is due. There is some good news, though. Alternate minimum tax does not apply to the final tax return.

REGISTERED PLANS: RRSPS AND RRIFS

Money contributed to a registered retirement savings plan created tax deductions for the contributor (except with overcontributions). That money has been growing—hopefully—in the RRSP or RRIF on a tax-deferred basis. When the annuitant of an RRSP or RRIF dies, the government wants to get back some of that income tax (and maybe even a little more!). Some people forget that they received tax deductions when they made their contributions and are incensed when it is taxed coming out.

Although the rules of RRSPs and RRIFs are slightly different, there are a number of similarities. When you die, your registered plan dies as well. RRSP money can be transferred to a spouse's RRSP tax-free. RRIF money can be transferred to a spouse's own registered plan, or RRIF payments can continue to be made to the surviving spouse if he or she was designated as the surviving annuitant. If the beneficiary is not a spouse, the money is cashed and the amount, less withholding tax, is paid to the beneficiary named on the RRSP or RRIF. If there is no named beneficiary, the money is paid to the estate. The estate is responsible for paying any additional tax due on the amount withdrawn.

NAMING YOUR BENEFICIARY

Who you name as the beneficiary affects the amount of tax to be paid on death, so be sure to keep your beneficiary designation up to date, especially if you divorce or remarry.

A Spouse

When a spouse or common-law spouse is the named beneficiary, RRSP or RRIF assets can be passed to them with no immediate tax due.

RRSP

When your spouse or common-law spouse is the named beneficiary, the assets in the RRSP can be transferred to his or her own registered plan (or a new plan if your spouse did not have one). The transfer is done through what Revenue Canada calls a refund of premiums, where the amount of the deceased's RRSP is included in the beneficiary's income *and* offset by an RRSP tax receipt for the same amount. This allows the registered funds to continue their tax-deferred status without affecting the spouse's own RRSP contribution limit.

Of course, your spouse has the option of withdrawing funds from the registered plan after the transfer and paying tax on the amount withdrawn. Better to leave the money in the RRSP if it is not needed, since it cannot be put back once it's withdrawn.

If you have an RRSP home buyer's loan inside your RRSP, the outstanding loan will be included as income on the final income tax return unless your spouse was named as the beneficiary on the RRSP and took out a home buyer's loan at the same time you did.

EXAMPLE

Barb and Manuel each took out an RRSP home buyer's loan for $15,000 to purchase their first house. Each named the other as the RRSP beneficiary. Five years later, Barb dies; she has $10,000 remaining on her loan. Manuel has two options.

1) Barb's $10,000 loan balance can be added to her final income tax return (even if the rest of the RRSP is rolled over to Manuel's RRSP), or

2) Barb's whole RRSP, including the loan balance, can be rolled over to Manuel's RRSP. His RRSP loan balance is now $20,000, since he also had a $10,000 loan balance. He will repay a minimum of $2,000 per year for the next 10 years.

RRIF

When your spouse is the beneficiary or the "successor annuitant" on a RRIF, he or she becomes the annuitant of the RRIF and receives the continuing RRIF payments. Alternatively, the RRIF can be transferred to the surviving spouse's own RRIF.

If the surviving spouse is under 70 and does not require the annual income from the RRIF, the RRIF can be converted back to an RRSP. This shelters the investment income from tax until the RRSP matures.

A Dependent Child or Grandchild

If you name as the beneficiary, a minor child or grandchild who was financially dependent on you at the time of your death, the registered funds can be used to purchase an income-producing annuity until the child is 18. By purchasing an annuity, the income from the amount withdrawn can be spread over a few years, resulting in less tax, if this meets your overall financial objectives. For example, if your RRSP is worth $60,000 at the time of death and your grandchild was 15, the amount taxed would be about $20,000 each year for three years, if an annuity was purchased, rather than $60,000 in the year of death.

If your spouse predeceased you and you do not have a young child or grandchild to name as the beneficiary, the entire amount is taxable in the year of death on the final tax return.

The Estate

If no beneficiary designation is made, the money in an RRSP or RRIF is cashed and paid to the estate. The full value of the registered plan at the time of death is added as income, on top of any other income you had that year, to the final income tax return.

If you do not have a spouse, common-law spouse, or children under 18, sometimes it is an effective strategy to name your estate as the beneficiary, particularly if the estate will need the money to pay bills or if you expect no other significant income to report in the year of death. (If only we could time this accurately!)

> What if you are survived by a spouse but did not name him or her as the beneficiary on the registered plan? If your spouse receives the proceeds under the will, he or she can elect to have the RRSP proceeds transferred to his or her own RRSP as a refund of premiums.

Q. I am a 65-year-old widower with an RRSP worth $100,000. My annual income is $45,000. I don't want my estate to have to pay that huge income tax bill on my RRSP when I die. Should I think about taking the money out of my RRSP now?

A. If you withdraw the entire amount from your RRSP now, you will pay tax on the full amount. If you leave it in the plan, your estate will pay tax on the full amount. If you need some funds consider withdrawing them now, but first look at how this might affect any seniors benefits you receive. A rule of thumb: you are better off leaving any money you don't require inside your RRSP to grow on a tax-deferred basis. Revenue Canada will get you now or later. I recommend it be later—you won't object as much then.

Someone Else

Careful tax planning is required when the beneficiary on your RRSP or RRIF is *not* a spouse, common-law spouse, or financially dependent child or grandchild. In that case, the market value of the plan is treated as if it was cashed in on the date of death.

The financial institution will pay the entire proceeds to the named beneficiary, less withholding tax. The maximum that must be withheld by the financial institution is 30%, which may not cover the actual amount of tax owed by the estate. The estate would have to settle the tax on the final income tax return, which would likely reduce the value of the estate for the beneficiaries named in the will.

EXAMPLE

Susan is widowed and has three adult children. To be fair, she wanted to leave each child an equal amount on her death. She planned to distribute her assets (all registered in her name) as follows:

To her eldest, $200,000 in cash through her will.

To her middle child, her home worth $200,000 through her will.

To her youngest, her RRSP worth $200,000 through the RRSP beneficiary designation.

But on Susan's death, this is what happened:

Her middle child received the house (no tax due because it had been Susan's principal residence).

Her youngest child received $140,000 from the RRSP ($200,000 less 30% withholding tax).

The eldest child received $160,000 (the $200,000 cash less the additional tax paid by the estate on the RRSP that was not withheld).

The result did not reflect Susan's wishes. If only she'd known and organized her affairs differently so each child could have received an equal share.

Q. I have a lot of strip bonds and stocks in my self-directed RRIF. My children are named as the beneficiaries (my husband died two years ago). Will these investments need to be turned to cash?

A. Not necessarily. If there is enough cash in your estate to pay the final taxes without requiring any funds from the registered plans, your executor can request the financial institution to re-register the assets into an open brokerage account.

An estate may face substantial taxes on assets and registered plans that are not left to a spouse. And if you do owe Revenue Canada, they would like cash. A good question to ask yourself is, "Will my estate have access to enough money, either through cash, insurance, or assets that can be readily sold, to pay the tax bill?" To preserve the assets in your estate, you may need to name your spouse as your beneficiary, or transfer assets with no capital gains to other beneficiaries or have enough liquidity (cash or assets that you are willing to sell) to pay the tax. If you do not expect to have enough cash and want to keep assets in the family, you might want to consider life insurance or rethink your estate plan.

Q. My only asset is my RRSP worth $100,000. I've named my sister as the beneficiary. Have I just beat the taxman?

A. No. If an estate does not have the money to pay the income taxes due on the RRSP, Revenue Canada would "ask" the beneficiary to pay the taxes on the amount received from the RRSP. Since you named your sister as the beneficiary, the financial institution would normally pay $70,000 ($100,000 less $30,000 withholding tax) directly to your sister. Revenue Canada will then approach your sister for the additional tax due. Let's hope she didn't spend it all!

If an estate does not have enough cash or assets that can be sold to pay the tax bill, Revenue Canada has the authority to go to those who might have received gifts prior to your death to find assets to pay the tax.

U.S. ESTATE TAXES

If you are a Canadian who owns property in the U.S., you are called a "non-resident alien." (It has a real friendly ring to it, doesn't it!) A non-resident alien could face estate tax on the market value of the U.S. property at the time of death. Property includes, but is not limited to, real estate, such as the condominium in Florida, and jointly held property.

Since 1988, Canadians who died owning more than US $60,000 of property in the United States were subject to U.S. estate taxes. Revenue Canada taxes profits on the assets and property up to the date of death, and these Canadians were required to pay U.S. estate taxes based on their total wealth (not just the profit) *in addition* to taxes due to Revenue Canada. This created a potential double taxation problem.

In 1995 the new protocol to the Canada-United States Tax Convention was ratified, and now Canadians whose worldwide estate is valued at less than US$600,000 may not be subject to U.S. estate tax. Canadians who hold assets or property in the United States receive some relief from double taxation when the deceased's worldwide assets are less than $1.2 million and a large percentage of these assets (including life insurance proceeds) are held in the United States. If a very small percentage of the estate's assets are held in the United States, there will be little tax relief under the new rules.

The new unified tax credit is based on the following formula:

$$US\$192,800 \; \times \; \frac{\text{value of assets in the U.S.}}{\text{value of worldwide assets}}$$

ESTIMATING YOUR U.S. TAX BILL

Table 6 was extracted from a U.S. tax return; all the figures are in U.S. dollars. The example that follows demonstrates how to use it to estimate a U.S. estate tax bill (the boldface numbers in the table are used in the example).

TABLE 6

A	B	C	D
TAXABLE AMOUNT OVER ($)	TAXABLE AMOUNT NOT OVER ($)	TAX ON AMOUNT IN COLUMN A ($)	TAX RATE ON EXCESS AMOUNT A (%)
0	10,000	0	18
10,000	20,000	1,800	20
20,000	40,000	3,800	22
40,000	60,000	8,200	24
60,000	80,000	13,000	26
80,000	100,000	18,200	28
100,000	150,000	23,800	30
150,000	**250,000**	**38,600**	**32**
250,000	500,000	70,800	34
500,000	750,000	155,800	37
750,000	1,000,000	248,300	39
1,000,000	1,250,000	345,800	41
1,250,000	1,500,000	448,300	43
1,500,000	2,000,000	555,800	45
2,000,000	2,500,000	780,000	49
2,500,000	3,000,000	1,025,800	53
3,000,000		1,290,800	55

EXAMPLE

Robert owned a condominium in Florida worth US$200,000. The estimated U.S. estate taxes due would be $54,600, calculated as follows:

Value of property held on the date of death	US$200,000
Tax due on first $150,000 (from column C)	$38,600
Tax due on next $50,000 (from column D)	$50,000 x 32% = $20,800
Amount of U.S. estate tax due before credit	$54,600

Since Robert's worldwide estate was valued at US$1 million, the tax credit would be calculated as follows (see formula on previous page):

$$\$192,800 \times \frac{\$\ 200,000}{\$1,000,000} = \$38,560$$

Amount of U.S. estate tax due by Robert's estate after the unified credit	$16,040

Note: Prior to the new treaty, Canadians received a deduction of $60,000 from the market value of U.S. property at the time of death. For example, U.S. estate tax would have been calculated on $140,000 for Robert's condo and more U.S. estate tax would have been due.

STRATEGIES TO REDUCE YOUR U.S. ESTATE TAX BILL

Non-resident aliens have used a number of techniques to reduce their U.S. estate taxes, including:

• Making small, regular gifts of U.S. property (although this is not practical if your only U.S. asset is a condo worth $150,000).

• Selling your property prior to death. If you no longer use the condo as much as you used to, or you anticipate your death (maybe you've been diagnosed with a terminal illness), you could sell the property while you are alive and move the proceeds back to Canada. If you don't own U.S. property at the time of your death, your estate will not pay any U.S. estate taxes.

- Holding U.S. investments inside a Canadian corporation. Some advisors recommend holding U.S. investments (but not personal real estate) inside a Canadian corporation, where the objective of the corporation is to hold personal-use property. The U.S. government may change its rules at any time and determine that assets held this way are not really corporate assets, limiting the effectiveness of this strategy.

- Leaving property to your Canadian spouse, since the new treaty provides an additional spousal credit.

- Making your estate worth less than US$1.2 million.

- Buying life insurance to provide the funds to pay tax due. But before proceeding, request a cost-benefit analysis projecting the tax bill and the cost of the life insurance premiums.

If your estate needs to write a cheque to the Internal Revenue Service, the IRS likes to be paid in U.S. dollars. The currency exchange rate at the time the cheque is written will affect the amount left over for your beneficiaries. If the amount owed is US$100,000 and your estate's liquid assets are in Canadian dollars, the executor would need to buy U.S. dollars to pay the bill. If the Canadian dollar is at 72 cents, the bill would cost the estate $138,000 Canadian.

> **T**
> **I**
> **P**
>
> The change to the U.S.-Canada Tax Convention is retroactive to November 10, 1988. Refiling the final U.S. return for deaths after this date could result in a refund of some of the U.S. estate tax paid under the old rules. Amended returns must be filed before November 10, 1996, or within three years of the deceased's original tax assessment, if later. In limited circumstances, some Canadians will be able to deduct part of the U.S. estate tax bill from their Canadian tax bill.

Canadians who are married to a U.S. citizen or who have dual citizenship have additional estate planning considerations and should consult an accountant who specializes in U.S. tax planning for Canadians.

If you own property outside Canada or the U.S., you may have an added complexity to your estate planning. Consult with your advisor to determine if you will owe tax in that country.

10

FILING THE FINAL INCOME TAX RETURNS

Your executor is responsible for filing the final income tax returns on time and ensuring that all the income taxes due to Revenue Canada are paid. The final income tax return for a deceased taxpayer includes all his or her income for the current year up to the date of death and is just like the tax return that you file each year. In addition, your executor is responsible for filing tax returns from previous years if they have not been filed.

Revenue Canada has a supplementary income tax guide called "Preparing Returns for Deceased Persons," available from the District Taxation Office. I've selected only some of the more commonly encountered rules for discussion here that we have not already discussed in Chapter 9.

DEADLINES

The due date for the final return and the tax payments depends on the date of death. If death occurs between January 1 and October 31, the final return is due by April 30 of the following year. If death occurs between November 1 and December 31, the final return is due within six months of the date of death.

Revenue Canada charges interest penalties on any amount owed that is not paid by the due date. In 1996, the late filing penalty was 5%, plus an additional 1% for each month the return was late to a maximum of 12%, or a total of 17%.

> **Ensure there is enough in your estate to pay the income taxes. Even if you distributed all your assets while you were alive so that there would be nothing of value in the estate to pay the final income taxes, Revenue Canada has the right to go to your beneficiaries to collect the tax.**

When income tax is owed on capital gains from the deemed sale of assets, the tax can be paid in up to 10 annual instalments. If there is limited liquidity in the estate, this can help to pay the tax bill over time without forcing an early sale of an asset at a poor time in the market. But your estate will still have to come up with the cash for each instalment *and* the interest due (non-deductible) on the amount outstanding for the privilege.

Q. *I am a widower and own a building worth $1 million. Since there is $800,000 capital gains on this building, will my estate be required to sell the building immediately to pay the income taxes due?*

A. I'll assume that the building is your only significant asset. It could be sold immediately if the price was right and there was a willing buyer. Alternatively, you could give your executor the power to hold the real estate in the estate until market conditions are right and pay the income tax by instalments. Your executor would do a cost-benefit analysis of the different scenarios, calculating the amount of income tax plus interest and penalties that would be due by instalments, and assess the market conditions for real estate in the area. After looking at the numbers, some executors may decide to sell the property sooner rather than later, to wrap up the estate.

Executors responsible for determining whether to sell or to pay by instalments may want to obtain the opinion of a certified real estate appraiser or other professional to ensure that they have acted in the best interest of the beneficiaries.

OPTIONAL RETURNS

Up to four tax returns may be filed for the deceased: the final return and three optional returns, depending on the types of income the deceased received. (Optional returns do not apply to everyone.) Since all the deceased's income can be included on the final return, an executor is not required to submit optional returns. But if optional returns apply, some of the personal tax exemptions and tax credits can be used more than once and result in less tax.

There are three types of optional returns.

A RETURN FOR RIGHTS OR THINGS

Rights and things are amounts due to the deceased at the time of death that had not been paid, including

- vacation pay, salary, or commissions earned
- investment income earned, such as a dividend that was declared prior to death, or interest from matured bond coupons that had not been cashed.

  Interest earned on a bank deposit, where the interest had not been posted to the account, is not considered a right or thing.

Alternatively, the income from rights and things on assets transferred to a beneficiary within one year of the date of death can be reported on that beneficiary's tax return if the income of the beneficiary is very low.

A RETURN FOR A SOLE PROPRIETOR OR PARTNER

If the deceased earned business income from a partnership or sole proprietorship with a year end that was not December 31, the executor can file an optional return for income earned from the last business year end to the date of death. Again, the income on the optional return may fall into a lower tax bracket, resulting in some tax savings.

EXAMPLE

> Lynn's dental practice had a year end of January 31. Lynn died on April 30, 1994. Her executor could choose to file a final tax return reporting 15 months of income, or two tax returns; a final return reporting 12 months of income for the period ending January 31, 1994, and an optional return reporting the business income for February 1, 1994, to April 30, 1994.

A RETURN FOR INCOME
FROM A TESTAMENTARY TRUST

If the deceased had been receiving income from a testamentary trust (a trust set up in someone else's will) with a year end that was not December 31, the executor can file an optional return for the trust income received to the date of death. Again, reporting this income on a separate return may result in less tax.

TAX RETURNS FOR THE ESTATE
AND TESTAMENTARY TRUSTS

In addition to the final income tax return and any optional returns, the executor is required to file an annual return (a T3 trust tax return) to report the income earned on any assets held in the estate from the date of death until the assets are all distributed, with a few exceptions.

EXAMPLE

> The deceased's $50,000 bank account is transferred to the estate. Before the account was distributed to the beneficiary, it received $500 in interest, which would be reported on the T3 trust return, not on the deceased's final income tax return.

The trust for the estate pays income tax based on graduated income tax rates (similar to an individual tax return) but is not able to claim any personal tax credits. The charitable donation tax credit is the only eligible tax credit for an estate.

Q & A

Q. My husband's estate existed for only a few months and everything was left to me. The estate earned $8,000 of interest income. Do I need to file a separate tax return for the estate?

A. No, you have the option of simply adding the income from your husband's estate to your own income tax return. However, if you have income of your own, you may be able to save some income tax by filing a separate tax return for the income earned during the "estate" period. For example, if your own income is $60,000, about $4,000 would be due on the estate income. If the $8,000 interest was filed on a separate return, it would pay very little tax.

It makes it worth filling out another government form for the estate, doesn't it? But an estate cannot exist just for income splitting. To hold the assets in trust for a beneficiary for a longer time, the will would need to establish a testamentary trust.

If the executor is named as the trustee for testamentary trusts established under the will, he or she will file separate income tax returns for these trusts. (See Chapter 13 on trusts.)

11

FAMILY LAW AND YOUR ESTATE PLAN

Each province has its own family laws to protect the rights of a spouse and dependants. Your legal and financial obligations remain your obligations after death and affect your freedom to distribute your assets. Lawyers refer to this as the "restriction on testamentary freedom." A dependant is defined as a person who relied on you for financial support immediately before your death and usually includes a spouse and dependent children. In P.E.I. and Ontario, a common-law spouse, parents, and grandparents are included in the definition.

SUPPORT AND MAINTENANCE

If your will fails to provide adequate support and maintenance for your dependants, they can apply to the courts to obtain an order against the estate for continued support. The legislation for support is found in such acts as the *Family Relief Act* (Alberta), the *Dependents Relief Act* (Manitoba), the *Wills Variation Act* (B.C.), the *Dependants of a Deceased Person Relief Act* (P.E.I.), and the *Succession Law Reform Act* (Ontario). Although the name and the wording of the act varies from province to province, the intent does not. In each province, the courts have the authority to order the estate to provide support to the dependants of the deceased (known as the testator). To give you an idea of how broad this wording is, here is part of the clause from the *Testator's Family Maintenance Act* of Nova Scotia:

> Where a testator dies without having made adequate provision in his will for the proper maintenance and support of a dependant, a judge, on application by or on behalf of the dependant, has powers, in his discretion and taking into consideration all relevant circumstances of the case, to order whatever provisions the judge deems adequate to be made out of the estate of the testator for the proper maintenance and support of the dependant, where the dependant means widow or widower or child.
>
> If a dependant contracts out his right to apply under this act, the promise is not binding on the dependant.

The order for maintenance and support may be made from income or capital in the estate and could be paid out as

- a monthly or annual amount for a limited or an indefinite time, or until a specific age or event, such as marriage
- a lump sum to be held in trust
- property to be held in trust for the dependant for a limited or indefinite time
- possession of specified property for life or a specified time
- any other way the court considers appropriate.

If an order is granted, it overrides the instructions in your will and can restrict the distribution of the estate.

Additional obligations may be found in a marriage contract or separation agreement.

COMMON-LAW RELATIONSHIPS

Under the federal *Income Tax Act*, common-law spouses have rights similar to married couples. Property, RRSPs, and RRIFs can be transferred to a common-law spouse and the income tax deferred until the death of the surviving spouse. Common-law spouses generally do not have any rights to property under family law, but they might have a claim for ongoing support.

SAME-SEX RELATIONSHIPS

Same-sex partners are not recognized by the legislation covering estate planning but we may see changes with the recent amendment to the *Human Rights Act*. Use of the word "spouse" in this book *does not* apply to same-sex couples. It is important for people in same-sex relationships to clearly indicate their intentions in their estate planning documents.

Q. My partner and I are in a same-sex relationship. Are we protected under family law?

A. In Ontario, a 1996 court ruling gave same-sex couples support obligations, but in other provinces, same-sex relationships have little or no protection. They are not treated as spouses by the *Income Tax Act*. There are no payments from Canada Pension Plan, disability pension plans, or most corporate pension plans.

To protect assets in same-sex relationships, be sure to name your partner as the beneficiary of your RRSP, pension plan, and life insurance, and prepare your will. Joint ownership of assets is another method.

DIVORCE

If you were divorced and providing spousal or child support through a divorce agreement, you may be required to continue support payment after death. Some agreements state that support ends with death. Other agreements might require you to maintain adequate insurance coverage to provide funds to continue dependent support after your death. Some agreements may not state anything. Failing to meet your obligations could override the instructions in your will.

MOVING

Family law is provincial. If you move, review your estate plan to ensure it reflects the family legislation of your new province. If everything is being left to your spouse and other dependants, you will likely not require any major changes.

MATRIMONIAL PROPERTY

Some provinces have laws that protect a spouse's right to a just and equitable distribution of property (including the matrimonial home) on death. In other words, the spouse cannot be written out of the will, or receive less than would have been received on divorce.

The executor can be held personally liable for any loss to the spouse if he or she fails to address a spouse's right to property on death.

The impact of these laws must be considered when preparing a will—otherwise the will can be overridden. Later in this chapter we will discuss how the laws work in Ontario.

> The executor of an estate could face personal liability if he or she fails to inform the surviving spouse of the right to receive an equalization payment. This could create a potential conflict for an executor who has the responsibility both to make decisions in the best interests of the surviving spouse *and* to follow the deceased's instructions.

MARRIAGE CONTRACTS

In most provinces, to protect the assets brought into a marriage, or to formalize your oral agreements and understandings, couples could prepare a marriage contract, or a pre-nuptial agreement.

If your province's family laws do not reflect your family or business needs, consider putting your intentions in writing. For example, you are marrying for a second time and you want to protect your business for your children. Set up your estate so that your instructions will be followed through a properly prepared will, marriage contract, or a living trust arrangement.

FAMILY LAW FOR ONTARIO RESIDENTS

This section affects residents of Ontario only. Ontario passed special family legislation in 1987. Neglecting family law in Ontario can create unnecessary stress on family relationships, delay the settling of an estate, and result in outcomes that were not intended. Regardless of when or where your will was written, if you die in Ontario, its family laws are applied to your estate.

Ontario family law states that property and assets acquired during a marriage are to be shared equally if the marriage breaks down; death is included as a form of marriage breakdown. The surviving spouse has the legal right to elect to receive the inheritance as stated in the will or, if left less than 50% of the net family property, to apply to the courts within six months (unless extended by the courts for special circumstances) to receive an equalization payment based on property held the day before death "as if they had separated." If an election is not made within six months, the spouse is assumed to have accepted the terms of the will.

Some spouses are reluctant to elect the entitlement even if it would be to their benefit. Making an election does not draw into question the state of the marriage. Rather, it reflects poor planning on the part of the deceased.

Q. I live in Ontario. My wife will receive a generous annual income from my estate. Is this enough?

A. Under the Ontario *Family Law Act,* a spouse may elect to take *either* the terms of the will or to receive an equalization payment. Your wife would determine if she is better off accepting the terms of the will or electing for the equalization payment. If she prefers to receive an outright lump sum rather than an annual income (however generous), she can so elect. If an equalization payment is elected, it takes priority over the instructions in the will.

THE EQUALIZATION PAYMENT

If your spouse does not receive everything under your will, he or she should weigh the value of the benefits that would be received under the will against the value of an equalization payment. Independent financial advice is recommended. To calculate the amount of an equalization payment, the value of net family property is calculated, in general terms, as the value of all property the day before the date of death

> *less* the value of property brought into the marriage, but not including the matrimonial home (the home and cottage used by you and your spouse)

> *less* the value of gifts or inheritances received during the marriage unless the money was used to pay off a matrimonial home

> *less* any income received from a gift or inheritance *if* there were written instructions from the donor to exclude it from net family property.

EXAMPLE

André's will leaves his wife, Lise, property and assets valued at $150,000. The net family property calculation at death indicates that Lise had $50,000 of net family property in her name and André had $450,000 in his name. Under Ontario family law, Lise is entitled to half of the net family property ($450,000 − $50,000) ÷ 2 = $200,000.

Since André's will leaves Lise assets and property valued at $150,000, Lise would be better off to make an election to receive the equalization payment of $200,000.

EXAMPLE

On Marsha's death, the family's assets and liabilities are:

TOM	MARSHA	
$150,000	$150,000	jointly held home
	$200,000	investment real estate
	$400,000	business where children are employed
	($100,000)	less value of business at the time of marriage)
0	0	less liabilities
$150,000	$650,000	family property held

In Marsha's will, investment real estate valued at $200,000 is left to Tom and her business is left to the children.

Calculation of equalization payment:
($650,000 − $150,000) ÷ 2 = $250,000.

Tom could elect to receive the equalization payment, which is $50,000 more than he would get under the terms of the will. Since the estate does not have sufficient cash to pay Tom the $50,000, his election could force the sale of the business, or he could become a reluctant partner in the business with the children.

But Tom and Marsha had agreed that Marsha's $500,000 life insurance policy would cover his needs.

The value of all property owned by either spouse the day *before* the date of death is included in the equalization payment. Consider what this means if you have provided for your spouse through life insurance and have left a significant asset, such as your business, to your children. Even if the life insurance might be worth more than the assets left to your children, it is *not* included in the value of the property owned the day before death. Without carefully worded documents, your spouse could receive the proceeds of a life insurance policy *and* elect to receive an equalization payment from the estate. While this is not bad for your spouse, it may not reflect your good intentions and could have a detrimental effect on the assets left to your children.

 If you are not planning to leave everything to your spouse, project the value of an equalization payment, and take any necessary steps so that your spouse does not need to make a claim.

In Tom and Marsha's case, Marsha might want to protect her business for the children and ensure her husband does not change her mind. In addition to wills, they could prepare a marriage or single-purpose contract to formalize their agreement so that the understanding is not left to the good will of the surviving spouse. Such a contract can be signed at any time during a marriage. Each spouse should obtain independent legal and financial advice to ensure he or she is not being coerced into "giving away" something, and make it more difficult to challenge the agreement later. You must also consider how realistic it is to expect your spouse to sign a marriage contract *after* you have been married for 20 years!

SUMMARY

Be sure to discuss with your lawyer how the law in your province affects your estate plan. I have discussed what can be complex issues in just a few pages.

12

Who knows what the future holds? When you buy life insurance, the life insurance company agrees to pay cash on your death to your beneficiary, in exchange for the premiums you pay. Life insurance is sometimes referred to as risk management: the risk you are managing is the financial impact your death would have on your dependants.

Simple Definition of Life Insurance
You pay. You die. Insurance company pays.

Before you buy life insurance, determine whether you— actually your dependants—really need it. Most people either need it or they don't.

Common estate planning uses for life insurance include:

- to create an "instant" estate so your family can be raised, educated, and supported. If you are divorced, you might be legally required to have life insurance to cover your support or maintenance payment responsibilities after your death.

- to pay off the mortgage or other debts. For example, you and your spouse can afford the mortgage payment as long as you both are working, but you don't want your spouse to have to sell the house if you die prematurely.

- to settle the expenses of your estate (including probate fees, legal fees, and U.S. estate tax) so no assets have to be sold
- to offset any taxes due to Revenue Canada so the assets in your estate remain intact. (See Chapter 9.)
- to pay for your funeral
- to provide cash so your business partner can afford to buy out your share of the business
- to make a more generous gift to charity than you might otherwise be able to afford
- to leave family members equal benefits from your estate. For example, if you plan to leave the cottage or business to one family member, you might leave other family members life insurance proceeds in a similar amount.

If you've decided you need life insurance, there are a few things to consider, such as how much, with whom, what type of policy, and what features or options the policy should have.

BUYING LIFE INSURANCE

HOW MUCH?

The amount of life insurance you require depends on your situation (the number and needs of your dependants and business partners), how much insurance you currently have, your current income, the assets you have, your debts, executor and probate fees, income taxes due on death, education funding, other sources of income your survivors may have, and some assumptions about the future.

When you look at buying a new vehicle, you have a sense of what your family needs. If you have to carry around your three children and the dog, you know a sportscar will not be appropriate (no matter how much you really want it!). Sit down and think about what your family's situation would be if you were hit by a bus tomorrow. Would your survivors have enough money to pay the bills, finish their education, or just have enough money to live on? Will there be enough money to create the income they require? Discuss this with your spouse; it might give you a better sense of whether there is a need.

The Canadian Life and Health Insurance Association has a booklet called "Sharpen Your Pencil—Life Insurance: How Much Is Enough?" which is available by writing to The Information Centre, Canadian Life and Health Insurance Association, 1 Queen Street East, Suite 1700, Toronto, Ontario, M5H 3S2.

Q & A

Q. How often should I review my insurance?

A. Insurance policies often just sit in a file somewhere gathering dust. As your family situation changes, or you change your employer and your group coverage, or the value of your investments changes, the amount or type of insurance you need may also change. Do you have too much? Is your insurance coverage sufficient? Like applying for a loan at the bank, the time to obtain it is before you require it. Be sure to review your insurance coverage every few years and when there is a significant change in your situation.

Buying life insurance is a matter of matching your needs with an appropriate policy. The amount of insurance you need when you're 40 can be very different from the amount you need at 60. If you require less insurance than you currently have, there are ways to reduce your coverage:

- Take out a new policy for a smaller amount. (Watch out though. A new policy could be more expensive because you're older or your medical health has changed.)
- Make an existing policy paid-up (if it has a cash value).
- Cancel it.
- Donate it to charity.

There are pros and cons to these options, so discuss them with your advisor to ensure that you don't face any adverse tax consequences and to determine what's most appropriate for you.

In order to buy life insurance, you need to apply for a policy. The life insurance company will assess your application and look at your medical history and other factors. If the insurance company accepts your application, it will issue a life insurance policy contract. You have the right to examine the policy to ensure it will provide the protection you require. As with any contract, be sure to read the insurance policy and ask for an explanation of anything you do not understand.

The financial stability of the insurance company, the features of the policy, the guarantees, and the cost are important considerations when selecting an insurer and a particular policy.

Q. Are there any guarantees that a life insurance company will pay up?

A. Under Canadian law, the insurance company has financial obligations to its policyholders. Insurance policies specify which situations are not covered (excluded) by the contract, such as suicide within two years of purchasing the policy. But if an insurance company goes bankrupt, Comm-Corp (Canadian Life and Health Insurance Compensation Corporation) protects policyowners for up to $200,000 of life insurance coverage per person at any one insurance company. To receive a booklet detailing the CommCorp Consumer Protection Plan, call the Canadian Life and Health Insurance Association information centre at 1-800-268-8099 (in the Toronto area, call 416-777-2344).

If you need more than $200,000 of life insurance coverage, you may want to consider splitting the amount between two or more companies to maximize the CommCorp coverage. The more companies you use, the higher your total premium will be (because each company charges a policy fee), but this can help to ensure the coverage is there when it is needed.

WHAT KIND?

Q. *What is the best type of life insurance?*

A. There is no simple answer. You want to ensure you purchase sufficient coverage with a quality insurer at a competitive price.

A number of insurance products are on the market, some of which make more sense in some situations than others. Life insurance can be broadly classified as temporary or permanent, with many policies being combinations and variations of these broad classifications. The name on a policy does not always indicate the type of coverage.

The cost of life insurance—the annual premium—is based on such factors as your age, sex, the amount of insurance applied for, the type of policy, special features such as cost of living indexing and guarantees, your health, whether you are a smoker, your hobbies (such as flying), the policy definitions, and the insurance company's pricing structure and assumptions about mortality rates. (The mortality rate is the company's calculation of the probability of death at any given age.)

If you were renovating your house, you would get more than one quote or put the job out to tender. To be a good consumer of life insurance, I recommend you obtain more than one quote for the coverage you require. (But don't delay too long. You don't want to expire before you get your life insurance in place.) Because product names and policy features vary from one insurance company to the next, compare the coverage based on the features you require. If the policy has features you don't require, you might be paying extra.

Term

Term insurance (sometimes referred to as temporary insurance) pays a specific death benefit for a particular period of coverage (the term). It provides the highest death benefit for the lowest premium, so you can get the maximum amount of insurance for the dollars spent. Term insurance is often referred to as pure insurance because there is no savings or investment component.

The price of term insurance increases each time the term of the policy expires. Each time the term is up, the insured is older and the probability of dying is higher, and so are the premiums. The premiums for a one-year term policy increase every year. Premiums for a 10-year term policy increase every 10 years.

Some contracts state that they are renewable at guaranteed premiums. Guaranteed premiums *does not* mean the premium will not increase. Rather, it means that the premium cost at any given age is guaranteed in the policy contract for the life of the policy. A 10-year guaranteed *renewable* term policy guarantees the premiums and that you have the ability to renew the insurance without producing evidence of good health every 10 years. With this type of coverage, the insurance company cannot refuse to continue to insure you regardless of your health in the future.

The most common estate planning uses for term insurance are to create an instant estate for a family and to eliminate significant debts.

Term to 100

Term insurance can be purchased so that the annual premium remains the same every year until a specified age. A term to 100 policy guarantees the premium cost with no increases until age 100. As an added bonus, if you live past 100 the premiums stop but coverage continues. (This may not be the case in all policies, so check your contract.)

Term policies are available where the premiums stay the same to other ages. The coverage (and the premiums) for a term to 75 policy ends at age 75. If you live to be 79, your beneficiary would not receive any money from this policy. With life expectancy increasing for both men and women, select a policy that will last as long as coverage is required.

Although a term to 100 policy is generally more expensive than pure term insurance in the early years, it can provide the next highest death benefit for the premium dollars spent. And because the premiums do not increase, the policyowner is likely to keep a term to 100 policy in force longer than a one-year term policy.

As another variation, some insurance companies have a term to 100 policy, or permaterm, that may provide some guaranteed cash values—if you keep the policy long enough. If you compare two term to 100 policies, the one with the cash value might be the better option if there is no significant difference in cost.

Whole Life

Whole life insurance is permanent insurance that combines insurance for your whole lifetime with a savings component. Premiums for whole life insurance stay level (that is, they do not increase), so you may keep the insurance in force longer than a renewable term policy. With a whole life policy, the amount of insurance coverage purchased with each dollar of premium is less than the coverage purchased for a dollar of term insurance.

A cash value projection will give you some idea of the future cash value of the policy, based on the assumptions used by the insurance company. But remember, there is a difference between a projection and a policy guarantee. The cash value of a whole life policy is available either as a policy loan while the policy is in force or as a cash payment if you cancel the coverage.

Some people compare the difference between whole life and term insurance to the difference between renting and owning. They do not like feeling they are "throwing away the premium payments" when they buy term insurance. They prefer whole life insurance because there is going to be something at the end of the day that is theirs. But life insurance is not like home ownership. If you select a policy because there is a savings component, rather than on the amount of insurance you need, you could end up being underinsured.

Universal Life

A universal life policy has a term insurance component and a tax-deferred savings or investment component. With a universal life policy, you contract for an amount of life insurance coverage, pay the base premiums, and possibly pay additional premiums for more investment or insurance. The cash component of the policy is invested in vehicles selected by the policyowner. Although the minimum death benefit is normally guaranteed, the cash value and maximum death benefit vary with investment performance.

A universal life policy is marketed as one that provides the flexibility to increase (subject to continued insurability) or decrease the amount of insurance as your situation changes. The premiums can be increased to maximize the savings component, or decreased or, as long as there is enough money in the savings/investment component, suspended (a premium "holiday") and the policy paid from the cash value.

> Compare the cost of the premiums for the universal life product with the cost of other insurance products. Look at the guarantees, if any, the projections for the savings side, and the size of any fees or charges. If you do not maximize the savings/investment side of the policy, or take lots of "holidays," this type of policy could be more expensive than term insurance over the long term.

NAMING A BENEFICIARY

On death, the policy death benefit is paid tax-free directly to the beneficiary named on the policy. If you indicate "Estate" as your beneficiary, the death benefit will be paid to your estate and be subject to probate fees. If you have creditors, they could make a claim on the life insurance proceeds once they are in your estate.

There are benefits to naming a beneficiary (other than your estate).

• The death benefit is paid directly to the beneficiary named.

• The amount is tax-free to the Canadian beneficiary.

• Payment is made quickly (usually within 30 days of submitting proof of death).

• Since the death benefit does not go through the will, it is not included in a probate fee calculation.

• The death benefit is protected from the deceased's creditors, except Revenue Canada.

The beneficiary designation on a life insurance policy may be revocable (it can be changed at any time) or irrevocable (it cannot be changed without the signed consent of the previous beneficiary). Irrevocable beneficiary designations are more often found in older policies.

It is important to keep the beneficiary elections up to date on all your life insurance policies, including any group policies. If you want to change your beneficiary, contact the life insurance company or your insurance broker. They may send you a beneficiary change form to complete.

To keep the money outside your estate, name an alternative beneficiary on your policy in case your first beneficiary predeceases you. For example, you may want your spouse to receive the death benefit. But if your spouse predeceases you, you may want your children to receive the death benefit in equal shares. If the children are minors, the money would need to be held in trust until they are old enough.

LIFE INSURANCE PREMIUMS VERSUS INCOME TAX

If you leave everything to your spouse, the income tax can be deferred until after your spouse dies, when the assets pass to the next generation. But if you outlive your spouse, or do not have a spouse, and have a cottage, RRSP, RRIF, an investment portfolio, or a business, you could be surprised by the amount of tax owed on the final tax return. RRSPs and RRIFs are treated as if they were cashed in and on other assets, all previously untaxed capital gains are taxed.

Now that the $100,000 capital gains exemption has been eliminated it is even more important to consider the income taxes due on assets that cannot be transferred tax-free so that particular assets, such as a cottage or business, can be preserved for your beneficiaries and do not have to be sold to raise cash to pay the taxes.

Q. I am considering buying life insurance to pay the income tax that will be due upon my death. Is the death benefit from a life insurance policy taxed?

A. No.

Purchasing life insurance to pay off tax and other debts at death is not a new use for life insurance; debts have always been part of the "how much do I need?" calculation. Estimating the amount of income tax to be paid at death is not an exact science—it's a moving target. But even a rudimentary calculation will give you a figure to work with. Then ask yourself whether you want to insure for it. For some people, the real question in this area is not "How much insurance do I need?" but "Do I want to pay insurance premiums each year?" and "What will happen if I do not purchase insurance coverage?"

Before purchasing life insurance to preserve the value of your estate for grown children, decide if it makes sense. If your children do not require the full value of your estate, you might not want to spend the money on insurance premiums.

JOINT LIFE INSURANCE POLICIES

A joint life insurance policy is a policy where the need for insurance is based on two lives. The cost (the premiums) is also based on the ages and health of two lives. There are two types of joint policies; joint second to die and joint first to die.

JOINT SECOND TO DIE

A joint second to die policy, sometimes called a joint and last survivor policy or joint last to die policy, pays out the death benefit after the death of the *second* insured. Nothing is paid to the beneficiary until after the death of both insureds, and the policy premiums are paid as long as one of the insureds is alive.

For example, the Smiths have accumulated a significant estate (house, cottage, and business) they want to leave to their adult children. Each has an RRSP on which they have named the other as beneficiary. Their other assets are registered jointly so that on the death of the first spouse all these assets will transfer to the surviving spouse tax-free. But on the death of the second spouse, they anticipate high bills for income tax, probate and legal fees *and* they want to keep the business and cottage in the family. The Smiths purchase a joint second to die insurance policy to provide enough cash to pay the bills so their estate can pass, intact, to their children.

If the purpose of the life insurance death benefit is to pay the deceased's income taxes, naming the "Estate" as the beneficiary ensures that the money is paid to the estate and is available for that purpose, unless there are creditors who have a claim against the estate.

The cost of this type of policy is usually cheaper for a married couple than a policy with the same death benefit for a single male the same age. A primary reason is that women are likely to outlive their spouses and the benefit does not pay until the second spouse dies.

To estimate the cost benefits of a joint second to die policy, base the cost on the number of years the premiums will likely be paid. Take Keith and Catherine, both 60, who are looking at a joint second to die term to 100 policy. The premium illustration they looked at assessed the cost benefits of the policy for 20 years, or in this case, until Keith reaches 80. But according to Statistics Canada, a woman Catherine's age has a 48% probability of being alive at age 85. So an illustration based on 20 years would underrepresent the possible cost if Catherine lives to be 85. You may want to ask for illustrations to age 86 or 92 if you feel that is more appropriate for you. Ideally, the cost of life insurance over your lifetime should be less than the amount of income tax to be paid.

When the purpose of the insurance is to preserve the value of your estate for your children, it has been suggested that you get them to pay the annual premiums, if you cannot afford them. This may be a good idea, but you'll have to discuss this with them and have them buy into the idea. In my experience, people generally don't want to discuss their affairs in detail with their children or discover the children don't have the money.

Some people say "it's not my problem" and will not want to pay life insurance premiums to offset the tax bill. You may well say "but my kids will get enough already, so why should I spend more?" There is no right or wrong answer. It's your money. You can do what you want. Do what makes good economic sense and fits your own belief system and your family's needs.

Q. I have no spouse. Is it better to let my estate pay the income tax on my RRSP or RRIF or to buy life insurance to cover the income tax bill?

A. It depends on a number of factors and your personal situation.
- Are you insurable?
- Can you afford the insurance premiums?
- What might the value of your RRIF be at death? Will it grow faster than you withdraw it?
- Do your children need the extra inheritance?
- Do you hate the idea of paying more tax, even if it costs you premiums while you are alive?
- Are there other ways to reduce the tax bill? For example, if you have no family and you want to leave everything to a registered charity, you could make the beneficiary on your RRIF your estate, and in your will make a bequest to the charity and receive tax relief on the charitable donation. (See Chapter 15.)

JOINT FIRST TO DIE

A joint first to die policy pays out the death benefit when the first insured dies. For example, two business partners buy a joint first to die life policy together. When the first partner dies, the surviving partner receives the insurance proceeds to buy the other's share of the business from the estate.

LIVING BENEFIT

Life insurance contracts state that the death benefit is payable only after proof of death. But some health conditions before death create such financial hardships that the reality is that the death benefit would be more of a benefit when the person is still alive. People who are terminally ill and who have life insurance may be able to receive some of the death benefit while they are alive—basically an advance on the insurance benefits of up to 50% (maximum $50,000) of the death benefit. Insurance companies call this a living benefit.

If a policy has been in force for at least two years and medical certificates state you are terminally ill and not expected to live more than two years, you might qualify to receive a living benefit. Some newer policy contracts state that a living benefit is available. If you find yourself in this situation, check with your insurance company—even if a living benefit is not expressly stated in your policy—to see if they have implemented this benefit.

Some terminally ill patients have sold their policies at a discount (sometimes a deep discount) to viatical companies in the U.S. In Nova Scotia and Quebec, Canadian LifeLine Ltd. is able to loan terminally ill patients money using their insurance policy as collateral.

13 ——— TRUSTS

"It is so hard to know if I am doing the right thing for my son. He's 20 now, and I don't know at what age he'll have the wisdom to manage all of my money. I have left everything in trust for him until he is 30 and have chosen trustees who understand my wishes. I hope I've done it right." L.

Trusts have been around for hundreds of years and can be used for a variety of purposes, but they all *entrust* a trustee with assets and property on behalf of others. They can be set up after your death (a testamentary trust) or while you are alive (an inter vivos trust). This chapter looks at what a trust is and some of the ways they can be used to achieve estate or tax planning or to meet a family need.

Although trusts are not for everyone, they have been used in situations that include

- managing money for children until they are older
- managing assets for a child or spouse who is unable to because of disability, age, or mental incapacity
- tax planning (although changes in tax rules have made this increasingly difficult)

- protecting assets from lawsuits and creditors
- income splitting with family members
- charitable giving
- reducing probate fees
- an alternative to a power of attorney document if your situation requires more formal instructions
- the need for privacy, since trusts are private, whereas assets flowing through the will can become a matter of public record.

In some ways, a trust document appears to handle the distribution of property and assets that could be handled by a will. In fact, a testamentary trust is set up in a will. However, there may be some situations where a person may wish to set up a trust while he or she is alive.

As with any financial strategy, you need to consider the pros and cons of setting up a trust. In simple situations, they may not be practical or cost effective. In other situations, such as a trust for a minor child or a disabled adult, the costs may be a secondary consideration.

Simply stated, a trust is a formal arrangement where the legal owner (called the settlor) transfers assets or property to a trust. A trustee is appointed to follow the rules of a trust agreement and manage the assets for the beneficiaries, who will ultimately benefit from those assets.

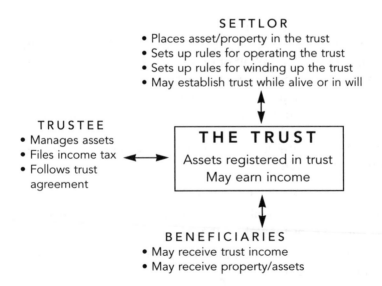

SETTLOR
- Places asset/property in the trust
- Sets up rules for operating the trust
- Sets up rules for winding up the trust
- May establish trust while alive or in will

TRUSTEE
- Manages assets
- Files income tax
- Follows trust agreement

THE TRUST
Assets registered in trust
May earn income

BENEFICIARIES
- May receive trust income
- May receive property/assets

THE TRUST AGREEMENT

The rules for a testamentary trust are written in the will. The rules for a living, or inter vivos, trust are written in a separate trust agreement, sometimes called a trust deed. The terms of the trust normally specify

- the purpose of the trust
- the assets to be put in the trust
- the beneficiaries of the trust
- the names of the trustees you are appointing
- the powers granted to the trustees
- what benefits the beneficiaries will receive from the trust and when
- how the assets of the trust will ultimately be distributed.

Trust law allows a great deal of flexibility, and as long as the purpose is legal, the terms of the trust can be as unique as your individual situation; as limited or as flexible as you require. Any areas not specifically covered by the trust agreement will be handled by your provincial trust laws.

To avoid tax and legal complications, the trust agreement should be prepared by an estate lawyer familiar with the type of trust you want to establish. If you require specialized expertise in this area, don't scrimp. The correct legal wording is extremely important. After a trust is established, changes to the trust agreement may be difficult, expensive, and sometimes impossible. A poorly worded trust agreement could end up costing you, or your beneficiaries, many more dollars in the future.

A trust could last for many years or the assets in the trust could be distributed according to the instructions in the agreement on your death or on the death of the last surviving beneficiary. If the beneficiaries are all over 18, they may request that the trustee distribute the trust assets prior to the provisions in the trust. This provides a mechanism to dissolve a trust when it serves no further purpose. (Caution: Beneficiaries should obtain independent financial and legal advice before requesting a trust be dissolved to ensure that they are not giving up any tax or legal advantage.)

BENEFICIARIES

The beneficiaries of a trust receive the benefit of the assets held in the trust, either now or in the future. Beneficiaries can be classified as income or capital beneficiaries, or both. In general, income beneficiaries are entitled to receive income (such as interest, dividend, or annuity income earned in the trust) and capital beneficiaries are entitled (or ultimately entitled) to receive capital from the trust (such as stocks, GICs, and real estate).

THE TRUSTEE

The trustee is responsible for managing the property held in trust and is required to

- manage and control the property according to the trust agreement and the provincial *Trustee Act*
- act in the best interests of all the beneficiaries
- perform duties with honesty, skill, and the highest level of care
- perform the duties personally and not to delegate the duties
- act without any conflicts of interest.

Trustees can be held personally responsible for any financial loss suffered if they do not carry out their responsibilities. Sometimes a trust agreement will state that the trustee is released from any financial liability as long as the trustee acted in good faith.

The trustee is required to act impartially and may have to make difficult decisions in the best interests of all beneficiaries. Consider a trust agreement set up for a spouse that states that after his or her death, any remaining capital in the trust is to be distributed equally among the children. One agreement could state the spouse is entitled to receive only the income earned by the trust. A different agreement could give the trustee full discretionary powers, including the power to give the spouse the trust income *and* any assets. These spousal trusts could result in different incomes for the spouse and very different estates for the children. In the extremes, the first agreement could result in the spouse receiving too little money to maintain his or her standard of living (because it depends only on the income earned by the trust). The second agreement could provide well for the spouse but might leave little to distribute to the children. As another example, Kevin and Eric are two child beneficiaries. Kevin needs additional money to pay for his education. Withdrawing funds from the trust for Kevin could be perceived by Eric as using up some of his own future benefits. To assist the trustee, the trust document should clarify the settlor's intentions.

The trustee you select might be a trusted family member or friend. Sometimes a professional trustee might be selected. A professional trustee, such as a trust company, can be a useful choice, especially if

- the assets to be held are particularly large or complex

- the trust will exist for a number of years

- specialized knowledge is required

- family members might have difficulty acting impartially.

As with most estate planning documents, name an alternate trustee. If your trustee dies and your trust agreement does not name a backup, then your trustee could end up being replaced by his or her executor.

POWERS OF THE TRUSTEE

A trustee's powers are authorized by the trustee act in your province (Civil Code in Quebec) and the trust agreement. You may want to draw up very specific instructions for the trustee in the trust agreement. If you want your trustee to have the broad power to distribute income and capital and make investment decisions as he or she sees fit, that must be specified in the terms of the trust.

Some people place the emphasis on selecting a good trustee. Then, rather than attempting to write instructions for every possible future situation, they give the trustee broad powers to make decisions in the best interests of the beneficiaries. Such full discretionary powers allow trustees to use their judgement to make decisions that are in the best interests of the beneficiaries. For example, if you are putting money in trust for your five-year-old today, you can't know how much a university education will cost 15 years from now. With discretionary powers, your trustee can pay out the required amount—and you don't have to stipulate an amount for 15 years in the future. Whether this strategy is appropriate for your situation depends on a number of factors, including who you appoint as trustee and who the beneficiaries are.

The trust agreement should provide your trustee with investment powers appropriate to manage the assets in the trust. A court ruling in 1994 suggests that a trustee or executor cannot hold mutual funds in a trust or estate. This ruling could affect Canadians who now hold mutual funds in their investment portfolios and suggests that if you want your executor or trustee to be able to hold mutual funds (including money market funds), you should explicitly authorize your trustee to do so. (This court ruling, I believe, is not a statement on whether mutual funds are good or bad but reflects the fact that mutual funds are not expressly referred to in trustee legislation and that legislation has not kept pace with Canadians' ever-growing acceptance of mutual funds as a way to invest. The decision is under appeal.)

TESTAMENTARY TRUSTS

A testamentary trust receives its instructions from the wording of the last will and testament. Clauses in the will name the trustee, the beneficiaries, what assets are to be held in the trust, and how they are to be managed and ultimately distributed. The cost of setting up a testamentary trust is included in the lawyer's fee for preparing the will. The terms of a testamentary trust are changed by simply updating the will, either with a codicil or by preparing a new will. (See the Chapter 4 for more details.)

Your estate is a type of testamentary trust, where the assets and property are held until they are distributed to your beneficiaries. Often, the trustee of a testamentary trust is also your estate's executor. But unlike your estate, a testamentary trust can exist for many years.

The common types of testamentary trusts are the spousal trust and family trusts. Family trusts include

- trusts for underage children who cannot hold assets directly

- trusts for spendthrifts, and
- trusts for family members with special needs.

SPOUSAL TRUST

A spousal trust holds property and assets for the exclusive benefit of a surviving spouse and may be established using some or all of the inheritance. Traditionally, spousal trusts were set up for widows who did not have the expertise to manage the assets they inherited. They now have several additional uses including:

- Income splitting when your spouse has an income. Assume half of your estate is left outright to your spouse and the other half is held in a spousal trust and that income is taxed in the trust. Each year, two income tax returns are filed, one for your spouse and one for the trust, which could result in less income tax being owed. For example,

> You have $100,000 of investments which earn $10,000 of income annually. If you leave $100,000 outright to your spouse, he or she may be required to add the $10,000 to his or her other income. Your spouse's taxes on the $10,000 would be $5,000 (assuming a marginal tax rate of 50%). But if you leave $100,000 in testamentary trust for your spouse, the taxe would be about $2,500 annually, resulting in a tax saving of $7,500 annually.

- To provide for your spouse *and* preserve the assets in the trust for your children in the event that your spouse remarries.
- To provide for your spouse and ensure that children from a previous marriage will receive something from your estate. A spousal trust could provide your spouse with an income for life, but on his or her death distribute the remaining assets to your children. This means that your children's inheritance is not dependent on the good will of a step-parent or the terms of the step-parent's will.
- To reduce probate fees. For example, if you leave your $100,000 bond portfolio to your spouse in your will, probate fees will be charged on those bonds. On the death of your spouse, probate

fees would be assessed a second time. If, however, on your death the bonds were held in a spousal testamentary trust until the death of your spouse, then they could be distributed to your children according to the trust agreement—avoiding a second probate fee.

Depending on the family or matrimonial property laws in your province, you might also require a marriage contract to indicate that your spouse consented to receive the inheritance in trust.

FAMILY TRUSTS

Trusts can be set up for family members other than a spouse, most often young children or children with special needs, or as part of tax planning. The wording in your will specifies the rules of the trust and they can be unique to your situation.

Trusts for Children

Children cannot legally own assets or property until they reach the age of majority. If they receive an inheritance, it must be held in trust until that time. If no trust is set up, the inheritance will be administered by the Official Guardian (the government) until the child is of age. Then the child would receive all the inheritance at once. Even if your child is old enough to legally own assets, how would you feel about your 18-year-old receiving a large inheritance outright—everything you have worked your entire life to acquire?

In your will you can set up a testamentary trust specifying when and how the money is to be distributed. The instructions might state, for example, that

- income earned by the trust is paid to the child annually but the capital is to be held until a specific age, with or without discretion for special needs

- all distributions from the trust are left to the trustee's discretion

- trust income and capital can be paid out at any time as long as it is used for education.

Q. *What if I don't want my children to receive their inheritance at 18?*

A. Your will could set up a testamentary trust to pay for their education and other expenses. There are many ways to set this up. For example, as each child turns, say, 25, that child would receive half of their remaining share and the other half at age 30.

Trusts for Income Splitting

Grandparents might want to leave money to their grandchildren for education or other expenses, rather than leaving the inheritance outright to their own, maybe more established, children. The grandchild's parent (your child) could act as trustee, if they can act impartially on behalf of the children.

Q. *I have three grandchildren for whom I wish to hold money in trust. Can I set up one trust for all three children, or should I create three separate trusts?*

A. You may do either. The purpose of three separate trusts would primarily be to file three separate tax returns and have each trust pay tax at the lowest possible tax rate. However, in the past, Revenue Canada has ruled that if the beneficiaries are in the same class, the income from these trusts must be taxed together.

Setting up a trust for grandchildren could provide some income splitting for the family. The income earned on the inheritance in the trust might pay tax at a lower rate than if it was left outright to the parent (for the children's benefit) and taxed at their higher tax rate. However, though in principle this is an effective strategy, I do not recommend it wholeheartedly. Your own children may be offended and feel left out even if they understand your reasoning. And remember, some parents believe their own children are better off than they really are.

EXAMPLE

Amount to be set aside for the grandchild $50,000

$50,000 held in a testamentary trust for child

Annual income earned in trust (at 10%)	$5,000
Annual cost of administering trust	0
Income of trust	$5,000
Income taxes paid by trust (federal and provincial)	$1,075
Net income of trust	$3,925

$50,000 left to parent outright on behalf of grandchild

Annual income earned in parent's name	$5,000
Taxes paid at parent's tax rate	$2,500
Net income on behalf of children	$2,500
Annual savings to family (parent/grandchild)	$1,425

Trusts for Children Over 18

A testamentary trust set up for children over 18 can protect assets from your children's creditors or from a divorce settlement. You might want to discuss with your children any liabilities they potentially face. For example, some professionals, including doctors, lawyers, and accountants, still register their home in the name of their spouse to reduce exposing their assets to creditors or lawsuits.

Depending on the amount, it might also create an opportunity for income splitting (similar to a spousal trust).

Trusts for Spendthrifts

A spendthrift trust, sometimes called a protective trust, is used to manage assets and property for people who may not be able to handle those assets if they received them outright. For example, your eldest son has been married twice and has declared bankruptcy. If you leave him the assets in your will outright, you feel they'd not last long. You could set up a testamentary trust to give him the income from the assets without giving him control over the assets.

Trusts for Family Members with Special Needs

A testamentary trust could be used to provide funds for beneficiaries who are financially dependent on you and are permanently unable to manage their financial affairs, because of disability or mental incapacity. This could include an ageing parent, or someone with mental or physical disabilities. For example, someone who is physically challenged may be able to earn an income, but his or her parents want to put money in trust in case he or she are no longer able to work and get around in the future.

Whether a person will be provided for adequately depends on the value of your estate, the assets placed in the trust, and how well the assets are managed.

If the family member is disabled and receives social assistance or a training allowance, an inheritance could affect his or her eligibility for assistance. If this is the case, discuss your options with a lawyer who has experience working with families in similar situations to see if the trust can be structured so it does not interfere with these benefits.

INTER VIVOS TRUSTS

An inter vivos trust is created during the settlor's lifetime and is sometimes called a living trust. Over the years they have been used for income splitting with family members and for financial planning. Now that the tax rules have been tightened up, inter vivos trusts are often used for estate planning when it is more appropriate to transfer assets to a trust while the settlor is alive, rather than through a will or a testamentary trust.

Inter vivos trusts can be used in estate planning

- to minimize the income taxes due on death, by freezing the value of investments or the shares of a business

- to provide privacy for your beneficiaries, since trust assets do not become a matter of public record

- to provide one individual with the use of the property, with instructions to transfer the property to someone else after death

- to minimize probate fees

- for charitable giving (see Chapter 15)

- as an alternative to a power of attorney, since a trust agreement can provide more detail and control over how assets are to be administered
- to protect the assets or property from creditors.

Q&A

Q. What is a revocable trust?

A. A revocable trust is a trust in which you retain the right to change your mind about having the trust and can have the assets revert back to you. The assets in the trust would not be subject to probate fees because, technically, the property in the trust belongs to the beneficiaries. A revocable trust can provide limited creditor protection if the creditors were not owed when the trust was set up.

With an irrevocable trust, you cannot change your mind and transfer the assets back to yourself. An irrevocable trust can have some tax advantages, but you give up personal control of the asset.

Living trusts can be revocable or irrevocable.

BEARER TRUSTS

Some assets are held in simple bearer trusts for children under 18; you might have set up one at the bank for your child. The registration on the account might read something like "Martha Scott in trust for Mary Scott," where Mary is Martha's daughter. Revenue Canada's attribution rules apply to these accounts. (See Chapter 6 for attribution rules.)

Because this type of "trust" does not have a trust agreement, it is not a formal trust. Legally, property in a bearer trust becomes the child's property when the child reaches the age of majority. If the amount held in trust is expected to be substantial, or you do not want the child to be able to access the funds until he or she is older, this is not the appropriate type of trust. Consider drawing up a formal trust agreement, setting out all the terms.

TRUSTS AND TAXES

The trustee is required to file a separate T3 tax return annually for the trust. Certain expenses of the trust are deductible. In most cases, the provincial tax rate paid by the trust is based on where the trustee lives.

TESTAMENTARY TRUSTS

When assets are transferred to a testamentary trust that is *not* a spousal trust, the tax on any capital gains from the "deemed" sale of those assets up to the date of death are paid on the deceased's final tax return.

When an asset is transferred to a testamentary spousal trust (as a spousal rollover), the tax can be deferred until the death of the surviving spouse, just as if the assets had been left outright to the spouse.

Ongoing Taxation

Income earned on assets held in a testamentary trust is taxed at graduated rates, just like the income of an individual taxpayer. When the income earned is low, the tax rate is low, when the income earned is high, the tax rate is higher. A testamentary trust cannot claim the personal tax credits, or any other non-refundable tax credits.

INTER VIVOS TRUSTS

When assets are transferred to an inter vivos trust, they are "deemed" to have been sold at fair market value. For example, if the value of the asset has increased, the settlor will have to pay tax on capital gains up to the time of the transfer.

Ongoing Taxation

The tax rules for living trusts are not as favourable today as they were a decade ago. Since 1985, changes to the federal *Income Tax Act* have limited the use of living trusts for income splitting with family members. Under Revenue Canada's tax rules for attribution, inter vivos trusts are more attractive when used for children over 18 than for those under 18.

All inter vivos trusts have a tax year ending December 31, and all trust income is taxed at the top marginal rate. This means that about half of each dollar of income earned in the trust goes to Revenue Canada. In 1996 an inter vivos trust with a taxable income of $40,000 would pay about $20,000 in federal and provincial income taxes. (A testamentary trust would pay only about $12,225.)

Prior to 1996, an inter vivos trust could have a group of beneficiaries classified as preferred beneficiaries. Under the preferred beneficiary election, income could be kept inside the trust and taxed as if it had been paid out to the beneficiary. If the beneficiary had little or no other income, there would be little or no tax due on that amount *and* the income could continue to grow in the trust.

As of 1996, the preferred beneficiary election has been eliminated, except for those beneficiaries who receive tax credits for mental or physical disabilities. For all other beneficiaries, the trust income now has to be actually paid out to beneficiaries to qualify for their tax rate. Capital gains and dividend income retain their tax-preferred treatment. For example, when the trust earns dividend income from a Canadian corporation and pays it out to the beneficiary, the beneficiary can declare it as dividend income and obtain the dividend tax credit.

If the trust was using the preferred beneficiary election, you might still be able to use the child's lower tax rate and retain control of the money if the trust income can be used to pay the child's education and other expenses each year.

21-YEAR RULE

After 21 years, trusts are required to report a "deemed disposition" of the assets at their fair market value. Tax is due on any profit resulting from this "sale"—ensuring that assets cannot avoid tax forever by being held in trust.

Trusts with preferred beneficiaries had been able to defer the deemed disposition until the death of the last preferred beneficiary, which could have lasted for generations. Starting in

January 1999, the deferral of the 21-year rule will be eliminated for family trusts with preferred beneficiaries, and tax will be due on profits.

 For trusts created earlier than 1979 where the trust assets have increased in value, determine with your accountant how best to plan for January 1999. You don't want the trust to face a generous tax bill and not have the cash to pay it.

In one extreme, ensuring that there is cash to pay the tax bill might require selling some of the assets before 1999. For example, a prominent family had established a family trust to hold a collection of Canadian antiques. The value of the collection had increased significantly but had been exempt from declaring any capital gains because of the preferred beneficiary election. The trust will face an enormous tax bill on the capital gain in 1999 and some of the antiques may have to be sold to pay the bill. Between now and 1999, the trustees plan to sell some pieces to minimize the tax bill and ensure that nothing has to be sold at "fire sale" prices.

In the other extreme, this change might mean distributing some assets outright to the beneficiaries before 1999. But first, review the reasons the trust was set up. Was it primarily to manage and control the assets? If so, then moving the assets out of the trust may not be desirable, since the trustee would no longer have direct control over the assets.

If the trust agreement does not give the trustee the power to adapt to changing tax realities, then the trustee might need to apply to the courts to formally change the terms of the trust (called varying the terms of the trust).

 Q. *What is an asset protection trust?*

A. An asset protection trust (APT) is a trust established to protect assets from creditors or a marriage breakdown. Since assets in a trust are technically outside your control, creditors cannot access these assets to settle your debts. But, if your creditors or estranged spouse can prove that you set up the trust to avoid your legal obligation, an asset protection trust will provide you with no "protection." Suggested minimums for an offshore APT are $250,000 (preferably $500,000 to offset set-up and administration fees).

COSTS FOR ESTABLISHING AND MAINTAINING A TRUST

There are fees for setting up trusts, legal fees, ongoing administration fees, and final distribution fees. If your province has written guidelines for fees, maximums are set according to the trustee act where the trustee lives. For a testamentary trust, the set-up cost is included in the cost of writing the will. For an inter vivos trust, the set-up cost includes the legal fees to establish the trust agreement.

The cost to establish and maintain a trust depends on the complexity of the trust, the value of assets to be held in trust, and whether you require a professional trustee. If the trustee is a family member, the trustee fee is usually waived. In general, assets of less than $100,000 would not be large enough to offset the cost of professional management. In fact, small trusts face a minimum fee for the services of a professional trustee, and this cost may be discouraging.

QUESTIONS TO ASK THE TRUSTEE ABOUT FEES ✓

Are there annual fees:

Yes No

❏ ❏ for preparing the income tax return?

❏ ❏ for managing the assets, based on the value of the assets?

❏ ❏ for the services of the trustee?

❏ ❏ based on the income earned by the trust?

❏ ❏ based on the money paid out of the trust each year?

❏ ❏ for distributing assets to the beneficiaries?

If "yes", ask to see the fee schedule and for an estimate of the costs that would be charged.

 Trustee fees can be negotiated, especially if the assets are of significant value.

The annual administration fee for a living trust with $500,000 in assets earning 10% annually might be calculated as follows:

Annual fee for preparing income tax return	$ 350
Annual administration fee (1/2 of 1%)	$ 2,500
Fee based on income earned (5% of $50,000)	$ 2,500
Annual total	$ 5,353

A final distribution fee might also be charged by the trustee when the trust ends and the assets are finally distributed to the capital beneficiaries. The fee depends on the value of the assets and the type of paperwork required to transfer ownership from the trust to the beneficiaries.

Even the public guardian, if required to act as trustee, is entitled to charge trustee fees, although for small accounts or for people on social assistance, the public trustee may waive its compensation.

DEALING WITH THE FAMILY COTTAGE

"What to do with the family cottage?" is something that you may have to look at. Families need to explore the various options, including setting up a trust, to find the solution that works best for them. Some strategies are designed to minimize the income tax that could be due on death. Other strategies are designed more around family wishes. The discussion that follows considers the advantages and disadvantages of some of the strategies.

First of all, if you would like to keep the cottage in the family, be sure to ask your children if they even want the cottage. It might not be as important to them as it was to you! For example, Liz and Dave have three adult children, two in Vancouver and one in Toronto. They could leave their Vancouver-area cottage to all three, giving each a one-third interest in it. But how much practical benefit would the cottage have to the child living in Toronto? It might be more equitable to leave the cottage to the two children in Vancouver and leave cash or other assets to the child in Toronto.

The cottage could be left to the next generation through your will in a number of ways.

- Bequeath the cottage to the children who want it and leave other assets or insurance to the others.

- Give the children the "right of first refusal" to buy the cottage from the estate.

- Leave your children an equal share in the ownership of the cottage. If your family gets along this could be effective. But what happens if one wants to sell his or her share but the others cannot afford to buy out their sibling?

- Place the cottage in a testamentary trust, which would protect it from the divorce or bankruptcy of a child. The trust agreement should set the rules to ensure fair and equitable use of the property and how operating costs are to be paid.

If there is a taxable capital gain on the property at the time of your death, the estate would be responsible for paying the tax. If your intention is to keep the cottage in the family, ensure that there is enough to pay the tax bill so that the cottage itself does not have to be sold.

In previous years, people used part or all of their capital gains exemption to minimize the tax on the sale of the cottage property. Now that the capital gains exemption has been eliminated, the following strategies are used to minimize taxes by those who believe the value of their cottage will increase. These strategies involve transferring the ownership of the cottage while you are alive and passing the tax on future profits to the next generation.

- If you are ready to give up ownership (and all the responsibilities that go with it), you could give or sell the cottage to the children at fair market value and you could hold a mortgage on the cottage to protect your own interests. Keep in mind, though, that life can be very different when you are the guest and your adult children are the owners.

- Transfer the cottage to an inter vivos trust but remember, trusts have to declare and pay tax on any capital gains every 21 years.

- Transfer the cottage to a holding company or non-profit corporation.

If the cottage has increased in value and there is a taxable capital gain from an actual or "deemed" sale when the property is transferred, you will be responsible for any tax resulting from the sale.

If you plan to sell your home and move into rental accommodation, a simpler strategy would be to elect the cottage as your principal residence. For the time the cottage is your principal residence, any increase in value would be exempt from income tax under the principal residence exemption.

And last but not least, do nothing now—except keep good records of any renovation costs.

SUMMARY

Professional advice is required to ensure that a trust is set up properly.

This chapter has touched on only some of the uses of trusts. A trust can be an effective tool to accomplish estate planning goals, but it can add cost and complexity.

14 BUSINESS SUCCESSION PLANNING

Just one question if you are a business owner: Will the business survive if you are not around? Not *can* it survive, but have you taken the time to plan so that it *will* survive on a sound management and financial footing?

In addition to personal estate planning, the business owner needs to ensure that the business remains in the family or goes to the intended people in such a way that it can continue to operate successfully. Most owners have worked too hard to leave the future of the business all to fate. Some of the estate planning issues for the business may be the same as the personal ones: to treat family members fairly, minimize tax on death, and have enough cash to pay those taxes. In addition to a will, the business owner may have to prepare shareholder agreements, obtain buy-sell insurance, and more sophisticated trust arrangements.

A change of management and taxation could make it next to impossible for a business to survive the loss of the key owner, especially if the business is in its first year or two. The more mature the business, the more chance it has to survive if proper plans are made. And remember, family business does not mean small business. McCain Foods, the frozen food company, is a family business.

Business succession planning—envisioning the future of the business without you—is difficult, but at some point it has to be done. Even the most successful business owner cannot run a business forever.

QUESTIONS TO CONSIDER ABOUT
THE FUTURE OF YOUR BUSINESS ✓

Evaluate your business situation.

Yes No Unsure

❑ ❑ ❑   Are you the business?

❑ ❑ ❑   Will the business be able to continue without you?

❑ ❑ ❑   Could the business be sold after your death as a going concern?

❑ ❑ ❑   If you have a spouse, does your spouse want to continue the business?

❑ ❑ ❑   If you have partners or other owners, can they afford to buy out your share?

❑ ❑ ❑   Do your children want to follow in your footsteps?

❑ ❑ ❑   Do any of your children have the aptitude for the business?

❑ ❑ ❑   Are you grooming your successor?

❑ ❑ ❑   Could any of your employees carry on the business?

❑ ❑ ❑   Will there be enough cash to pay the income taxes?

❑ ❑ ❑   Will the business have to be sold?

These can be difficult questions, questions that might have no clear answers. But the very survival of your business and the needs of your family depend on you working through these issues with your advisor.

Some of these same questions need to be addressed when you plan your retirement.

Should you consider "key man," or "key person" insurance? Key person insurance is insurance used to provide the cash to replace the services provided by a key individual in the business, on his or her death. Would you like your survivors to be able to hire someone to manage the business on your death until it can be sold or someone groomed to take it over? Of course, if the business has sufficient financial reserves, this person's salary might be funded from investments held inside the business, rather than from key man insurance.

SELLING THE BUSINESS

If you do not believe the business would survive your death, you may want to plan your retirement and possibly sell the business. If you are the primary asset of the business, the business would likely have a higher sale value while you are alive and able to help a new owner get established (maybe through a management contract). Giving up control is often a difficult decision, and this suggestion may be good only in theory, especially if the business is your main purpose in life.

If you sell the business but do not receive the full sale price in one year, you may be able to claim a capital gains reserve, which allows you to match the amount of taxable capital gains with the amount you receive each year (for up to five years after the sale). For example, you might sell your business for $300,000 and receive the sale price in instalments over three years. In year one, the amount of capital gains declared would be $100,000 and the remaining amount would be held as a capital gains reserve reducing over the next two years. You might also structure a retiring allowance with the sale to transfer the maximum allowable amount tax-free to your RRSP.

KEEPING IT IN THE FAMILY

Your business may be your single largest asset. Who will operate it as a going concern? Do you plan on dividing it among your family members? Leaving everything to your spouse? Leaving the business equally to all your children, or to just one? Although you may want your children to work together, it doesn't happen this way in most families. If one child runs the business, he or she may have different objectives than the children who are not-so-silent partners.

If your intention is to treat all your children as equally as possible but only one will be inheriting the business, you might equalize the benefits to those who are not active in the business by

• naming them the beneficiaries on life insurance

• leaving them personal or non-business assets

• leaving them non-voting shares in the business, or

• some other way that fits your family and personal situation.

If your spouse is not interested in running the business and the business is your primary asset, you need to determine how to adequately support your spouse. You may have heard of situations where the spouse of the deceased became an active partner in the business—much to the dismay of the other partners—because of inadequate estate planning for support or family laws.

POTENTIAL FOR FAMILY CONFLICT

Take the case of two brothers, 25 and 20, and two sisters, 23 and 18. Their father died at 50, having started a business four years earlier, leaving a spouse, a little life insurance, and some debts. There was not enough to provide an income for his widow, and the only family asset was the growing business. Since selling the company would have generated little cash, someone needed to step in and run the family firm.

There was no succession plan—indeed, it would have been difficult to have had a clear plan given the ages of the children at the time. The widow started working in the business, and the eldest son and daughter pitched in, but the eldest son had other career aspirations. Over time, the other two children tried to help out, but one did not have the aptitude for the business and the other found it difficult to work with his family and left.

Ten years later, the widow retired, and her "pension" today is dependent on the continued operation of the business. The eldest daughter and her husband are still successfully running the firm. The other three children, who are not active in the operation, still see "Dad's" business as part of their rightful entitlement.

This case has much of the intrigue of a soap opera: misfortune, fate, luck, ambition, conflict, and success. If this was your business, how would you want it handled? Should the son-in-law be rewarded for his major contribution with a partial ownership in the business? Or should he be treated as just another employee? Should all the children share in the profits, even though one child was clearly responsible for building and nurturing the company? How should the children share in the success of the father's vision?

Clearly, there are no easy answers. It doesn't matter if the business is a family campground, a french fry company, a successful retail operation, or a garage.

TAX PLANNING

If it is your wish to keep the business in the family and its value has grown, you need to estimate the income taxes that would be due from a "deemed" sale of the business on death. If you leave the business to your spouse, you have not eliminated the need to plan—you've just postponed the tax bill until the death of your spouse.

As with all financial planning, reducing taxes should not be the driving motivation when looking at what to do. First, you have to decide what you want to have happen. Then, by considering the tax rules, you may be able to structure the plan to minimize the tax bill—the icing on the cake, so to speak.

ESTATE FREEZES

An estate freeze is an estate planning strategy used to minimize the income taxes due at death. A number of techniques can be used, all focusing on locking in the value of an asset at a point in time and passing future growth or profit to the next generations. An estate freeze works best for assets that are expected to increase in value.

Transferring assets to an inter vivos trust is one of the most common techniques to create an estate freeze since you can retain some control over the management of the assets. Selling or gifting an asset to adult children will also lock in today's value. You might trigger an estate freeze by transferring your business assets to a holding company or doing a corporate reorganization.

> **If your business is a small business corporation, the sale of your shares in the business may qualify for the $500,000 capital gains exemption. Consider an estate freeze to lock in, or crystallize, the future tax savings from the $500,000 capital gains exemption.**

Performing an effective estate freeze is complex and requires professional financial, tax, and legal advice. In my opinion, anyone considering an estate freeze should regard it as permanent since it is difficult and costly to reverse (although it may be technically possible). You want to be sure that you do not create any adverse income tax implications today and that you have considered all aspects of any technique.

To satisfy Revenue Canada, it is important to get an independent valuation of the fair market value of any property, asset, or business for audit purposes.

When considering an estate freeze, ask yourself:

- Does your business have good growth potential?

- Are you psychologically prepared to give up control of the business and pass it on to the next generation? If you are actively building the business, you may not be ready yet to give up the benefits of your efforts.

- Will an estate freeze create a capital loss or gain and result in any immediate tax consequences?

- Is there an appropriate time to do an estate freeze? When the market value of the asset is low, there could be less immediate tax consequences.

- What are the legal and accounting costs? Are the benefits greater than the costs?

An estate freeze may work to reduce the income tax due on death, but this should not be the *only* reason. It also has to make good business sense!

ESTATE FREEZE THROUGH A HOLDING COMPANY

Transferring assets from an old corporation to a new holding corporation, in exchange for preferred and common shares of the new company, can create an estate freeze.

Typically, the parent/owner would hold the preferred shares and the children would hold the common shares. All future growth in the company would then occur through the common shares held by the children. (If they are minors, the shares would be put into a trust.) The holder of the voting preferred shares could still control the company, and the value of the company is not changed.

ESTATE FREEZE BY REORGANIZING A CORPORATION

Another way to create an estate freeze is to reorganize the share structure of an existing company (sometimes referred to as a section 86 freeze). The shares of one type are exchanged for another type. For example, the common shares of a business would be reorganized into two new classes of shares, the preferred shares and the common shares. The business owner would hold enough preferred shares (with voting rights) to maintain control of the company. The next generation would hold the growth shares of the company.

In some cases, the reorganization of a business is accomplished with some combination of estate freezing techniques including but not limited to

- transferring an active business to a holding company (under section 85 of the *Income Tax Act*), and

- using the remaining shares to reorganize the business capital so that after the estate freeze the children hold the growth shares and the parent holds the preferred shares.

NEEDS OF BUSINESS PARTNERS/SHAREHOLDERS

The death of a major partner or private shareholder can represent a major risk to the future of the business and the surviving partners and shareholders. In addition to the issues a family business faces, the person with partners or shareholders has some other questions to address.

- Under what conditions would the business continue?

- Would there be enough cash flow to operate the business?

- If your main asset is the business, will your family members be joining the partnership?

- Are your partners or shareholders willing to welcome your spouse or children into the business? Would you be willing to accept theirs?

- If your business can be run only by a professional, what arrangement should you make? A physician, for instance, might want to arrange with another doctor to take over the practice by some business agreement, or take on and groom a younger doctor.

- Can any of the business assets be sold to provide for your family so that they do not need to be actively involved in the business?

Although this chapter focuses on estate planning for your family and business partners or shareholders, you might also want to consider these issues should one of your partners or shareholders predecease you. Do you want the first rights to buy out their shares, or are you willing to have their family members become your partner or shareholder? In many cases, it makes sense for the surviving partners or shareholders to purchase the business interest rather than a stranger or competitor. The terms of such an arrangement would be found in a shareholders' or partners' buy-sell agreement.

The value of the business is not easily determined. It is based on a number of factors, including the market value of the business, the financial position of the business, and earnings potential according to some formula.

There may be an independent valuation of the business—to put a price on it. The remaining partners or shareholders would have to some way acquire the business at a fair price from your estate. A buy-sell agreement could be funded through

- the partners' personal cash or corporate reserves. Often, the personal funds will not be enough. A more mature business may have built up reserves inside the business to provide all or part of the necessary funding.

- buying out the deceased's interest with a loan to the spouse if the business can afford this expense annually until the debt is paid. Under the *Ontario Family Law Act,* a surviving spouse is entitled to a minimum of 50% of the value of the family assets, up front, if they elect. If your partners cannot afford to buy out your interest, they may end up with your spouse as an active, if unwilling, partner in the business.

- borrowing the funds. The loss of a partner/shareholder often represents a major risk to the future of the business and a bank manager may be uncomfortable loaning a large amount with a key individual no longer involved. You know it is easier to borrow money when you don't really need it!

- using life insurance to buy out the estate's interest in the business, or

- some combination of the above.

Once determined, the value of each shareholder's interest should be reviewed periodically to ensure that the other shareholders still have the ability to finance the buyout of a deceased's share.

PARTNERSHIP AGREEMENTS

A partnership agreement documents the rules for operating the business partnership, including how partnership assets will be transferred on the death of one of the partners. From an estate planning perspective, it should specify a buy-sell agreement, who will buy out the deceased partner's interest in the business, how the price will be determined, and how and when the proceeds are to be paid.

SHAREHOLDERS' AGREEMENTS

A shareholders' agreement documents the rules between private shareholders and covers many areas of the business agreement, including how a shareholder's shares in the business will be handled on the death of that shareholder. At a very minimum, a buy-sell agreement should specify who will buy the business or the shares, how the price of the deceased's interest in the business will be determined, and how the proceeds are to be paid.

Using Insurance to Finance a Buyout

If life insurance is determined to be the most viable option to finance a buy-sell agreement, there are two major ways to use it.

- If there are two principals in the business, each would purchase an individual policy on the other's life sufficient to buy out his or her interest in the business in the event that one individual predeceases the other. Because individual insurance is based on the health and age of the person being insured, one principal could end up paying more for this coverage than the other.

- Use corporate-owned insurance and have the business pay the premiums. On the death of one of the principals, the corporation would use the insurance to buy the deceased's portion of the business from the estate. Again, because this insurance is generally based on the health and age of the person being insured, an insured who is much older or in poor health may receive a greater premium "subsidy" from the corporation than the other shareholders. If this is not considered fair, you could work out some formula to equalize the subsidy.

Q. *Is it better for the corporation to pay the life insurance premiums or for me to pay them personally?*

A. Sometimes the discussion of whether the premiums should be paid by the individual or the corporation centres around which is the more tax-effective. But the corporation can ensure the insurance premiums are paid. Some businesses choose to pay the premiums because individuals sometimes forget.

A key to a successful business is planning. To maintain a business after death, the partners and executor need to know enough about the day-to-day operation of the business to keep it up and running. And partners and shareholders should have the cash to buy out the deceased's share.

The death of a key individual in a business can be difficult to plan for, but without estate planning and professional advice, the continued success of a business is uncertain.

15

GIFT PLANNING

"I have tried to teach people that there are three kicks to every dollar: one when you make it ... two, when you have it ... and three when you give it away."
paraphrased from William A. White, writer (1868-1944)

You might want to give to a particular charity in return for some help you or someone close to you received, or because of some affiliation you had with that organization. For example:

- someone who received a scholarship many years ago might want to set up a scholarship fund
- someone who has been helped tremendously by a hospital might want to give some of their estate to the hospital in gratitude
- someone who enjoys the arts may want to make a donation to an arts group
- someone whose family had been affected by a disease might want to fund research.

People also make gifts because they want to do something for their community, or because it gives them personal satisfaction, or because of religious convictions.

It is a reality of our times that charities and communities will be increasingly less dependent on government funding but will have more work to do, which takes money. Gift planning involves making charitable donations to get the maximum tax benefits. There are many opportunities to make charitable donations—with tax savings as a bonus—that can be built into an estate plan. In 1996 the federal budget increased the tax incentives for those considering a planned gift.

Gifts can be made while you are alive, deferred until after death, or a combination. Planned gifts can be made using cash, stocks or bonds, life insurance, artwork or manuscripts, real estate, or other assets of value, if they are acceptable to the charity. A cash gift or life insurance could be made today or promised for the future. Even some gifts promised for the future can have tax incentives today. Assets could be given outright or through a legal structure, such as a trust, corporation, or private foundation. Some of the strategies in this chapter work for gifts of any amount; some work better for larger gifts.

MAXIMIZING THE TAX
BENEFITS OF GIFT PLANNING

Saving taxes is usually not the first consideration when you make a planned gift, but saving taxes sure doesn't hurt. It goes without saying that the larger the gift, the more important it is to maximize the available tax benefits. Tax planning can help to determine how you can get the maximum benefit from a gift. It should not deter you from making a charitable gift or bequest.

To issue a valid tax receipt for a gift (an official donation receipt), the charitable organization or foundation must be registered with the Ministry of National Revenue and have a charitable number.

The amount of the receipt depends on the market value of the gift at the time the gift is made. If the gift is a financial asset (such as stocks, bonds, or the cash value of an insurance policy), the value is easy to determine. If the gift is personal property (such as art or manuscripts) worth over $1,000, it should be appraised independently to support the amount of the receipt. If the value of a gift cannot be determined, no charitable receipt can be issued. Whenever the gift is not cash, you should discuss it with the charity and confirm the amount that will show on the charitable receipt before you make the gift.

Revenue Canada does not issue a refund cheque specifically for charitable donations. Instead, the amount of tax saved is a non-refundable tax credit, which reduces the total tax bill for the year. The tax credit in 1996 is 17% on the first $200 of donations in the year and 29% on any amount over $200. The tax benefit is not as small as you might think. The donation saves both federal and provincial tax and any surtaxes that might have been due. For example, a charitable donation of $1,000 would reduce income taxes by approximately $399.

Amount of Tax Credit for Charitable Donations	
Total amount of gift	$ 1,000
First $200 of charitable donation ($200 at 17%)	$ 34
Amount over $200 ($800 at 29%)	$ 232
Federal tax credit	$ 266
Provincial tax credit*	
(assuming 50% of the federal amount)	$ 133
Total amount of tax saved	$ 399

* The provincial tax rate varies across Canada

The total charitable donation you can claim for the non-refundable tax credit while you are alive in any one year is limited to 50% of your net income, except for gifts to foundations (see "Gifts to Foundations" later in this chapter). In years when your net income may be low, the unused part of the donation can be carried forward for up to five years.

EXAMPLE

Louise made a charitable donation of $60,000 in 1995. Her net income for the year was $50,000. The maximum she could claim as a charitable donation for the non-refundable tax credit in 1995 was $25,000. Assuming her net income for the next four years will continue to be $50,000 annually, she would be able to claim the whole amount of the charitable donation over three years. But if Louise died in 1996, a portion of the tax benefit might go unused.

If the gift is made at the time of death or through your estate, the donation that can be claimed for the credit is up to 100% of your net income. Any unused amount cannot be carried forward (since this is the last income tax return), but your executor can apply the unused donation to your income tax return for the previous year (up to the 100% limit for that year).

> Spouses can pool their charitable receipts on one income tax return even if the receipts are not in both names. Having one person use all the receipts and claim the full amount could maximize the tax benefit, since $200 of the combined total would be calculated at 17% (rather than $200 for each spouse).

WAYS TO MAKE PLANNED GIFTS

GIFTS OF CASH

Every year, many Canadians give cash or write a cheque or have a donation deducted directly from their paycheque. The donation might be made at the office or through one of the various campaigns or events that charities use to raise funds throughout the year. The gift may be planned or unplanned. This is the simplest way to give and it allows the charity to benefit immediately. Most charities do not give receipts for donations under $10.

GIFTS THROUGH A WILL

The most common type of planned gift is a bequest made in a will. Up to 100% of the donor's net income can be claimed as a charitable donation in the year of death (and the preceding year, if necessary). While you may be tempted to leave all of your money to charity and not to your family, this wish is limited by the family or succession laws of your province. Lawyers call this a restriction on testamentary freedom. Governments see this as a way to keep your family off public support. Common sense calls this living up to your family obligations. However, some donors may have no family to leave their estate to and may elect to leave their entire estate to charity.

 Review your will and your charitable intentions. A charitable donation through your will might offset some of the taxes due on death.

Table 7 lists some types of bequests that might be made in a will. The wordings here are not the full legal wordings; many charities will provide your lawyer with sample language to add to your will to properly document your wishes.

TABLE 7

TYPE OF BEQUEST	SAMPLE WORDING
Gift of a specific sum of money	
• for general use	"I give A the sum of $ ___ to be used for general purposes."
• for a specific use	"I give B the sum of $ ___ to be used for (purpose)."
Gift of a specific asset	"I give C my collection of ___."
Gift of all/or part of the residue	"I give D 30% of the residue of my estate."
Contingent gift	"In the event my spouse does not survive me, I give E ___."
Trust remainder bequest	"I give X what's left in the trust after the death of the last beneficiary of the trust."

Tax benefits

Most gifts qualify for a charitable tax receipt. (If the gift is not cash, check with the charity.)

Other considerations

Works for gifts of any value
Probate fees could apply
Gift is not confidential
Relatively easy to change
Gift could be contested if you do not provide adequately for certain family members

GIFTS OF OTHER ASSETS

Real estate, stocks and bonds, and other valuables can be donated through your will or while you are alive, if they are acceptable to the charity. This type of gift is called a gift in kind, which just means it's not a cash gift. Unless there are restrictions to the contrary, the charity can manage the assets as it sees fit and determine whether it is appropriate to turn the gift into cash by selling it. This can save the donor or the estate from having to deal with the sale.

When the gift is something other than cash, technically, Revenue Canada treats the charitable gift as a "sale" of the asset or property for income tax purposes. If the market value of the item is more when the gift is made than when you acquired it, this profit will need to be reported on your income tax return. The taxable gain on an asset used to make a charitable donation is reduced by a tax credit.

EXAMPLE

Bob has a net income of $80,000. He donates 3,000 Bank of Montreal shares worth $100,000 to a registered charity. He paid $20,000 for those shares.

Capital gain on the gift

Market value at the time of the gift	$100,000
Cost of shares	$ 20,000
Capital gain	$ 80,000
Taxable capital gain (75%)	$ 60,000

Amount of gift that can be claimed in current year

Net income before taxable capital gain	$ 80,000
Taxable capital gain	$ 60,000
Total net income	$140,000
Amount eligible for charitable donation (50%)	$70,000

However, the taxable capital gain is offset by a $30,000 tax credit on taxable capital gain. The tax cost of making the charitable donation is 0. In addition, Bob can claim the tax credit on the remaining taxable capital gains and unused charitable amount over the next four years.

Project your net income for the year you plan the gift. If you plan to make the gift while you are alive and cannot use the entire donation in one year, claiming the remaining charitable donation over the next 4 years could still have tax advantages.

GIFTS THROUGH LIFE INSURANCE

A charitable gift can be made of a life insurance policy that you no longer need or by taking out a new policy. Using a life insurance policy has some advantages:

• the amount of the gift may be larger than you might otherwise afford

• if privacy is important, the gift can be kept outside the will.

Following are some of the more common options.

Changing the Beneficiary

One way to use life insurance is to name the charity as the beneficiary on the policy so that the death benefit would be paid directly to that charity. Although this strategy would avoid probate fees on the amount of the gift and provide confidentiality, just changing the beneficiary does not provide any tax benefits, since it is not considered a charitable donation by Revenue Canada.

Say you have a life insurance policy with a death benefit of $10,000 and no cash value; you want to leave $10,000 to your local hospital and receive the maximum tax benefit. One option is to name the charity as beneficiary on the life insurance policy.

Tax benefits

None, since insurance proceeds do not qualify for a charitable tax receipt.

Other considerations

No probate fees
Gift is confidential
Gift is difficult to challenge
The previous beneficiary might have to give signed consent. (See Chapter 12.)

Another option is to name your estate as the beneficiary on the insurance policy *and* bequeath a similar amount to the charity in the will. This would maximize the tax benefits related to the donation of the policy *and* retain the right to change the bequest in the future. The hospital would get the $10,000 and your estate would receive a tax receipt for a $10,000 charitable donation.

Tax benefits

The estate can use the tax receipt to offset some income tax on the final tax return.

Other considerations:

Probate fees are due on the amount that flows through the estate (which is usually a minor consideration compared to the potential tax savings)
Gift is a matter of public record if the will is probated
Gift could be challenged

Assigning an Existing Life Insurance Policy

If you have an old life insurance policy you no longer require for your personal needs, you could gift the policy to charity while you are alive, rather than cancelling it. The charity would receive the life insurance proceeds on your death.

EXAMPLE

Brian has a whole life policy with a death benefit of $25,000 and a cash surrender value (cash value less an outstanding loan) of $10,000. He assigned the policy to the charity and named the charity the beneficiary. The charity issued an official tax receipt for $10,000. Brian decided to continue to pay policy premiums so he receives an additional tax receipt each year for the premium payments.

When you absolutely assign a life insurance policy (that is, transfer the legal ownership) to the charity *and* make the charity the beneficiary of the policy, you are entitled to receive a tax receipt for a charitable donation for the cash value, if any, of the policy at the time of assignment. If the policy has no cash value (such as a term policy), no charitable receipt is issued for the gift. If the policy has a cash value, it may not be necessary to continue to pay premiums. If premiums are required to keep the policy in force after it has been assigned, the premiums paid each year may also qualify as a charitable donation.

Tax benefits

Official tax receipt for the cash value of the policy at the time of the transfer.

If premiums continue to be paid, they qualify for an additional official tax receipt each year, if approved by the charity.

Other considerations

No probate fees
Gift is confidential
Gift is difficult to challenge
Change is impossible to undo

> **T I P**
>
> If the policy had an unpaid loan when it was assigned, and you later consider paying it off, the *Income Tax Act* states that you qualify for an additional tax receipt. From a practical perspective, it would be just as easy to write a cheque directly to the charity. Then the charity would have access to the money immediately and you would still have an additional tax receipt.

Purchasing a New Policy

You can also make a charitable gift by taking out a new life insurance policy.

The cost for the insurance, like any other insurance policy, depends on a number of factors, including your age and your health. If you are considering this option, be sure that you can afford the premiums and shop around for the best rates from quality insurers. Some charities can help you arrange this directly through their own insurance programs, or you can arrange it through your life insurance representative. It has been my experience that charities prefer policies that build cash values or are paid up in just a few years if they are asked for charitable receipts.

Tax benefits

Official tax receipt for premiums paid in the year, if approved by charity.

Other considerations

No probate fees
The cost of the policy
Gift is confidential
Gift is difficult to challenge

GIFTS TO FOUNDATIONS

Crown Foundations

Although Crown foundations are relatively new, many universities, museums, hospitals, libraries, and other quasi-government agencies have this charitable structure.

When a gift is made to a registered charity, the amount that can be claimed for the non-refundable tax credit in any one year is limited to 50% of the donor's net income while alive, and 100% on death. But when a gift is made to the Crown (the government) or a Crown foundation, the limit increases to 100%. This allows you to claim the amount as a charitable donation for the year, up to 100% of your net income. From the donor's perspective, making a gift to a related foundation is the same as making a gift directly to the charity—except for the larger tax advantage while you are alive. For example, a gift to the University of Toronto is eligible for up to the 50% net income limit if made while you are alive, whereas a gift to the University of Toronto Foundation is eligible for up to 100%. However, a gift made through the will to either would be eligible for up to 100% of your net income.

Community Foundations

The mandate of a community foundation is to enhance the quality of life in the local community. There are more than 50 community foundations in Canada and more than 500 in North America. The Vancouver Community Foundation (established in 1942) and the Community Foundation for Greater Toronto (established in 1983) are just two examples of community foundations that support the arts, education, health, social services, and/or the environment in their communities.

A gift to a community foundation would be eligible for the non-refundable tax credit for up to 50% of your net income while alive; up to 100% if made through your will.

In addition to accepting donations of cash, other assets, and life insurance, community foundations are able to set up relatively inexpensive trust funds for scholarships or memorials.

GIFTS TO THE GOVERNMENT

Gifts of Ecologically Sensitive Land

Environment Canada considers ecologically sensitive land important for the preservation of Canada's environmental heritage. If you own such land, and fail to donate it to a Canadian municipality or to a special registered charity dedicated to conserving and protecting our environmental heritage, you face a tax penalty of 50% of the value of the land when it was disposed.

Gifts of Cultural Property

If you donate certified cultural property of "significant benefit to Canada" to a designated public institution (such as a public art gallery, historic site, or museum), that public institution may issue a charitable receipt, which you can claim for up to 100% of your net income and be exempt from capital gains.

Cases of abuse and fraud related to gifts of cultural property have been uncovered and Revenue Canada is being vigilant in this area, especially in cases where the value of the gift increases significantly in a short time. If you are considering donating cultural property, you must contact the public institution of your choice to determine whether the gift meets the criteria of providing a "significant benefit to Canada."

Other Gifts to the Government

Want to help pay down the country's debt? If you want to write a cheque to Revenue Canada and indicate that it is gift. Up to 100% of your net income can be claimed as a charitable donation.

OTHER TYPES OF GIFTS

Another type of gift allows the donor to continue to receive income or to use the asset *even after* it has been donated to charity. These gifts are made through a gift annuity, a charitable remainder trust, or a gift of residual interest.

This type of gift is promised today but is completed in the future. The amount that will show on the tax receipt is based on the projected value of the gift at the time of death. This residual value is based on a number of factors, including the current market value of the gift, current interest rates, and the current ages of you and your spouse. The older the donor is at the time of the gift, the greater the tax advantages. If the value of the residual interest cannot be determined, then no official receipt can be issued.

As with all of the strategies described in the book, discuss the benefits and the tax implications with your advisors, and be sure that your own needs are met, before you sign anything.

Gift Annuity

With a gift annuity, you give the charity a gift of cash, investments, or real estate in exchange for a guaranteed income for life. The charity (or an insurance company) invests the funds, and upon your death the charity receives any remaining value in the annuity. In many ways, a gift annuity is similar to an annuity issued by a life insurance company, except that the amount left over goes to the charity, not the insurance company.

The income you receive can provide attractive after-tax income, since some of the payment is considered a return of your own capital. The amount of guaranteed income is based on actuarial calculations, and depends on the value of the gift, your age, interest rates at the time of purchase, and any options you request. The income from an annuity is typically guaranteed for the rest of your life, or for the lifetimes of both you and your spouse under a "joint and last survivor" option.

A number of charities can issue their own annuities, or the charity can reinsure the policy or refer you to an insurance company. See if the charity of your choice requires a minimum gift to set up an annuity; some have very low minimums. And ask for a quote indicating the monthly income that would be available from the gift, the portion of the monthly amount that is tax-free (generally, the older you are, the higher this portion), and the amount of the charitable tax receipt.

The key with a gift annuity is the amount of after-tax income you require (otherwise, you'd probably make an outright gift of cash). If the income quoted is not sufficient to meet your current and future income needs, then this is probably not the right option for you at this time.

Charitable Remainder Trust

A charitable remainder trust is a way to transfer assets or property to a trust that allows you and your spouse continue to have the right to use the property or to receive all income earned by the property. On your death (or your spouse's death, whichever is last, if you want this option), the charity receives the "remainder" of the assets in the trust outright.

A charitable remainder trust is actually an inter vivos trust to which you irrevocably transfer property. Because you give up control of the asset, you can receive a tax benefit. The tax receipt is based on your current age (the older you are, the bigger the receipt), the asset being gifted, and actuarial projections of the value of the asset when the charity would receive it outright. Once the trust has been set up, you cannot change your mind, even if you need additional money.

As with any trust, the value of the assets to be held should be large enough to justify the costs of setting up the trust and the annual administration and trustee fees. For practical purposes, the value of the asset should be greater than $100,000, otherwise the related fees may be high enough that another method of gifting would be more appropriate.

This type of gift is less common in Canada (but it is growing in popularity) than in the United States where the U.S. taxpayer has to pay a wealth tax based on the value of the property they hold at death. The less property Americans hold, the lower their estate tax. (The term property is used in a very general sense. It could be cash, investments, or real estate.)

Charitable Remainder Trust

Benefits to you and your estate
Tax receipt now for charitable donation
Assets in the trust are not subject to probate
Continuing income or use of the property for the rest of your life
Beneficiaries cannot contest the trust
Can be tailored to your own situation
Confidential, since the gift is outside the will

Disadvantages to you
You lose control of the asset
The trust is irrevocable
Annual administration and trustee fees

Benefits to the charity
Receives title to the property
Knows the gift will eventually be received outright

Gift of Residual Interest

A gift of residual interest is created when you transfer the owner-ship of property to a charity, but retain the right to use the property (rather than receive income) according to a formal agreement with the charity. For example, you might gift your home, but you and your spouse retain the right to live in it for the rest of your lives. This can be great in theory, but many people do not feel comfortable giving away the home that provides them with a sense of security. Be clear about your emotional need to own the asset outright, especially if it is your home. Never give away something you are not prepared to give up, even if it is in name only.

This type of a gift also works for other types of property.

Gift of Residual Interest

Benefits to you and your estate
Tax receipt now for charitable donation
Assets are not subject to probate

Continuing use of the property outright for the rest of your life

Confidential, since the gift is outside the will

Disadvantages to you

You lose control of the asset

The gift is irrevocable

Benefits to the charity

Receives title to the property

Knows the gift will eventually be received

THE PROCESS OF GIFT PLANNING

Before giving to a particular charity, ensure that it has a charitable number registered with Revenue Canada. If you are unsure, Revenue Canada will confirm whether or not a charity is registered. You might want to ask the charity how much of the donation goes directly to the programs of the charity and how much would be used in administration. Unfortunately, there have been scams by unscrupulous charities.

If the donation is not a cash gift, ensure that the charity can use the gift you are considering. Many charities can provide you with sample language that your lawyer can add to your will to properly document your wish. Some of the larger charitable organizations have staff dedicated to assisting potential donors with their decisions. You should never feel that you are being pressured to make a donation during these discussions.

You might want the charity to use the gift as it sees fit, or you might have some specific ideas on how you want the gift to be used. If you have any instructions or conditions regarding how the gift is to be used, obtain the approval of the charity to prevent technical problems down the road. Restrictions may make it hard, and sometimes impossible, for the charity to accept the gift in the future, so check with them first. For example, if a charity does not receive the gift for several years and you have restricted the use of the gift to a particular program only, what happens if that program does not exist when the gift is eventually made? Even if you have a specific use in mind, consider giving the charity the right to use the gift in a more appropriate way at the time, so that it can be adapted to changing needs and be the most use when it is received.

Some charities have ways to recognize donations (such as placing the donor's name on a plaque), with the donor's permission, even when they might not receive any benefit until after your death. Having your name recognized can help others to consider making their own contributions, but it is not a requirement. Your gift can be made privately if you wish, but if the gift is made in your will, remember that a probated will becomes a matter of public record.

When naming a charity in your will or in a life insurance policy, use the full legal name of that charity. There are more than 72,000 registered charities in Canada, and some have similar names. You want the right one to receive the benefit—and not leave your estate with a dispute to settle.

SUMMARY

While saving taxes may not be the prime motivation for making a planned gift, there can be significant financial benefits.
   When planning the gift, be sure to consider

- the needs of the charity or charities you wish to assist

- ways to maximize the tax deduction

- the financial needs of your family, and

- your own financial needs so that you don't give away too much too soon.

   It is important to many people to know that they have made a difference.

16
DOCUMENTS CONCERNING HEALTH CARE

"I was responsible for my mother right to the end and I had to make some tough decisions. I discussed the options with my sister, but she refused to be involved in the decisions. I did the best I could for Mom, but to this day, even though I know I made the right decisions, I feel guilty."

"If my mother had let me know what she wanted, it would have helped. But it still would not have made it easy."   S.

In some situations, science and medical technology sustain life, but they may not be able to provide the quality of life you desire. Advance health care directives, included living wills, power of attorney documents for personal care, and health care proxies.

The legal status of these documents varies from province to province. For example, British Columbia, Ontario, Manitoba, Nova Scotia, and Quebec have legislation recognizing living wills. *The Substitute Decisions Act* in Ontario gives the legal right to prepare a living will and appoint a substitute decision-maker for health care (either as part of a power of attorney for personal care, or as a separate document). British Columbia has legislation that recognizes living wills and health care proxies and is moving to incorporate these into the Representation Agreement.

LIVING WILL

If you are mentally competent, you have the right to refuse medical treatment. However, if you become mentally incapacitated or unconscious, you are assumed to have given consent to all medical treatment that the medical establishment considers necessary.

A living will is misnamed: it is not a will and it deals with your dying, not your living. The living will indicates your wishes regarding the types or degree of health care or medical intervention you would like to receive or refuse when you are unable to speak for yourself. It does not provide another person to represent your decisions—for that you need a power of attorney for health care. The more clearly you indicate your wishes, the easier it will be for your health care providers to follow your wishes in the spirit you intended.

Some living wills include wording similar to "If it is anticipated that I cannot enjoy a reasonable quality of life after recovery or remission, I request that I be allowed to die and not be kept alive by artificial means or heroic measures." For example, it is a good idea to specify what you mean by "quality of life," such as not wanting to live hooked up to machines when there is no hope of survival.

Someone with a terminal illness might want to suffer as little pain as possible and indicate in their living will that they are willing to receive drugs to minimize the pain and discomfort, but that they do not want aggressive treatment or have their life sustained by artificial means. If you watch any of the medical shows on television today, you may hear actors and actresses facing terminal illness say "DNR" or "I'm DNR all the way." DNR stands for "do not resuscitate."

A living will documents your instructions for the refusal or consent to medical treatment. If, for example, you want to be an organ donor, you should make it clear that you can be left on a ventilator for that purpose.

> Discuss your beliefs and wishes with your health care providers. The more specific you can be (without being overly detailed), the more they will be able to respect your wishes.

The Dying with Dignity Association provides information and counselling services and also sells a living will form. They can be contacted at 188 Eglinton Avenue East, Suite 708, Toronto, Ontario, M4P 2X7; (416) 486-3998.

A living will needs to be signed by you, dated, and witnessed by people who believe you are mentally competent.

Q. Must my physician follow the instructions in my living will?

A. Yes and no. According to the Centre for Bioethics, the Canadian Medical Association supports living wills in principle. But some professionals may be reluctant to follow advance directives on medical treatment when those instructions involve assisting with a suicide, for fear of being charged under the Criminal Code.

The lack of legislation has not stopped the courts from recognizing living wills as valid documents. Even if you live in a province where a living will is not yet formally recognized, putting your wishes and beliefs in writing provides guidance to your family and medical professionals during difficult times. After all, the purpose of a living will is to provide direction to your family and your health care professionals regarding your medical care and the quality of life you desire.

Like other estate planning documents, a living will or advanced care directive should be reviewed regularly and updated if necessary to reflect your current wishes and medical condition. It should also be reviewed if you move to another province, as the provincial laws vary.

The Dying With Dignity Association recommends you review your living will annually and initial and date it when you do so. Your doctors can then be sure that the document still reflects your wishes.

POWER OF ATTORNEY
FOR PERSONAL CARE/PROXY

In some provinces, you may appoint someone to make decisions for your personal or health care on your behalf. This person may be called a health care proxy, representative, or a power of attorney for personal care. Naming a power of attorney means that someone of your choice—not a government official—has the right to make personal care decisions for you when you cannot. This document is different than a power of attorney for financial matters (see Chapter 8).

As with any personal representative, the person named should be someone you trust, who understands your personal values and will follow your instructions or, if you have not left detailed instructions, will make decisions based on what they believe is in your best interest and stand up for your wishes. If you name more than one attorney, they are required to make decisions on your behalf together, unless you state that they may act jointly and severally.

Even without a power of attorney for personal care, immediate family members may be able to make health care decisions on your behalf. Unlike financial matters, close family members can step in, especially in medical emergencies. In the forthcoming law in British Columbia, without this document, family members will be granted temporary authority to make these decisions. Health care facilities, such as long-term care residences and nursing homes, seem to be moving in the direction of requiring this type of document, even when a family member could technically act without it.

In Ontario, under the *Substitute Decisions Act,* the power of attorney for personal care can incorporate a living will and the attorney to make personal and health care decisions for you (hence "substitute decisions"). The attorney for personal care does not have any authority to make these decisions for you unless they reasonably believe that you are no longer capable of making a required medical decision yourself. To help prevent potential abuses, several groups of people who have certain relationships with you are excluded from being able to act as your attorney for health care decisions, including your teachers, doctors, nurses, landlord, or social worker.

In British Columbia, the pending legislation will enact the Representative Agreement, which gives your representative the authority to make these decisions (to "represent" you) and you the ability to name a third party to monitor the decisions the representative makes, unless you waive the requirement.

SUMMARY

Provincial legislation for advanced health care directives is evolving. Law makers are attempting to balance the needs of all involved to

- give the patient the power to make their own medical decisions

- give individuals the right to appoint someone to make decisions

- provide those named as substitute decision-makers with the legal authority to follow those instructions, and

- provide a legal framework that protects all parties involved, including the individual, the medical providers, and government officials who may become involved, without unnecessary red tape or high administration costs.

No one knows what the future will hold. My husband has the following words in his living will:

> Death is as much a reality as birth, growth, maturity, and old age. It is the one certainty of life. If the time should come when I can no longer take part in the decisions for my own future, I hereby direct that this statement be allowed to stand as an expression of my wishes made while I am mentally competent.

If the situation should arise where my attending physician(s) has determined that there can be no recovery by me from a physical and/or mental disability and that my death is imminent, I hereby direct that I be allowed to die. It is my desire not to be kept alive by artificial means or heroic measure which would only serve to artificially prolong the process of dying. I do not fear death itself as much as the indignities of deterioration, dependence, and endless pain. I request that I be allowed to die naturally with only the administration of medication and the performance of any medical procedures deemed necessary to provide me with comfort and/or to alleviate suffering, even though this may hasten the moment of my death.

This request is made after careful consideration. It may appear to place a heavy responsibility on those individuals in whose care I am in. However, it is with the intention of relieving you of such responsibility and placing it wholly upon myself in accordance with my strong personal convictions that this statement is made.

These words will provide me, and his doctors, with guidance, if he is ever in such a situation.

17
THE FINAL GIFT

"How do you say thank you?"   M.

On your death, you may want to donate your body for medical research or your organs to someone who desperately needs help. We each have to consider our own values and personal issues for this individual decision.

ORGAN AND TISSUE DONATIONS

You may wish to donate your organs or tissues to help someone who might otherwise die. An organ transplant can greatly improve the life expectancy and quality of life of the recipient. Today, kidneys, livers, hearts, lungs, pancreas, and small bowels are transplanted. The number of organ transplants performed is limited by the shortage of donors.

Tissue donation involves transplanting human tissue (rather than entire organs), such as bones for those who have lost large amounts of bone due to cancer, heart valves to replace faulty ones, and corneas for those whose sight has been damaged. Organ donors can also be considered for tissue donations.

Q. *Will my family know the names of the people I helped?*

A. No. The names are not released. However, your family will receive a letter within a few weeks informing them which organs and tissues were transplanted. There may be an option of communicating with the recipients by anonymous letter, and families are encouraged to initiate this correspondence.

To be considered an organ donor, the person must be declared brain dead by two independent doctors but still have a beating heart. Brain death is the end of all brain function and is irreversible. Because the donor is on a ventilator and the heart is still beating, the body's organs continue to receive oxygen and stay functional. Although we would like to think all donations can be used, the suitability of a donor's organs and tissues for transplant depends on the donor's health at death, and the cause of death. A signed donor card is legal consent, but doctors still get permission from the family.

Q. *When can the body be released to the family?*

A. After the declaration of death, the organ donation process generally takes up to 24 hours: 8 hours for the medical tests to be completed, 2 to 8 hours for the surgery to remove the organs (leaving no visible disfigurement), plus 8 hours if an autopsy is required.

Even if you donate your entire body to a medical school, your eyes can be donated for transplant but not your organs. Contact your local office of the Canadian National Institute for the Blind (C.N.I.B.) for more information on the Eye Bank of Canada.

SIGNED DONOR CARDS

Each province runs its own organ donation and transplant program, and maintains a database of people who are waiting for a transplant. While Canada does not have a national program, the provincial programs coordinate their services.

To indicate that you would like to be an organ or tissue donor, sign an organ donor consent card or the consent form on the back of your driver's licence, or state this in your documents for health and personal care. If you do not have a driver's licence, you can obtain a consent form from your province's transplant program. (See Table 8.)

| | At the time of death, decisions regarding organ donation need to be made quickly—delays can result in the organs being unusable. Carrying a signed organ donor card means your wishes are known immediately. |

If you have signed an organ donor card, it is easier for your family to carry out your wishes. Discuss your wishes with your family to help them understand, since a close family member may also be required to sign a consent form at the time of your death.

TABLE 8

ORGAN TRANSPLANT CENTRES

For more information, contact the centre closest to you. For general information, please call during office hours. After hours, calls from people who have an immediate need to refer an organ or tissue may be answered by a person on call, an answering service, or a message with an after-hours number to call.

Alberta
Southern Alberta	(403) 283-2243
Northern Alberta	(403) 492-1970
after hours, call Southern Alberta number	

| British Columbia | (604) 877-2100 |

| Manitoba | (204) 787-7379 |

New Brunswick	(506) 643-6848
Newfoundland	(709) 737-6600
Northwest Territories	call the closest provincial centre
Nova Scotia	(902) 428-5500
after hours call 1-(800)-565-0733	
Ontario	1-(800) 263-2833
London	(519) 663-3060
Hamilton	(905) 522-4941
Kingston	(613) 548-7811
Ottawa	(613) 737-8616
Toronto	(416) 340-3587
P.E.I.	(902) 428-5500
Quebec	
Montreal	(514) 286-1414
after hours call	(514) 286-0600
Quebec City	(418) 845-4110
Saskatchewan	(306) 655-1054
Yukon	call the closest provincial centre

Organ and tissue donation are ways to give something, even in death. It may be a way to ease some of the pain that occurs with a death, a way for something positive to come out of even the most tragic deaths.

DONATING YOUR BODY FOR MEDICAL RESEARCH

"Here lie the cremated remains of those who, in the interests of their fellow man, donated their bodies to medical education and research."

from a stone in the University of Toronto
section of St. James' Cemetery

You may wish to donate your entire body for education or scientific research at your local medical, dental, or other health profession school. But not all bodies offered are accepted. The school may already have enough, or there may be medical reasons for not accepting a body. Sometimes, the body is simply too far from the school for the donation to be practical. In case your body is not required, consider alternative arrangements, such as burial or cremation.

If your body is accepted by the school, the school will normally arrange for transportation of the body, but the estate or family will be required to pay for the cost.

The school will keep the body for between six months and three years. When the body is no longer required, it is cremated. Different schools have different options available after cremation. For example, at the University of Toronto, the cremated remains may be released to the family or the estate for a private burial (at the expense of the family or estate), or they may be buried by the university at the university burial service held each spring. For more information, contact the school in your area.

If your body is accepted for medical research or education, many people believe that it is still important for those close to you to recognize that a death has occurred. Family and friends may wish to hold a memorial service around the time of death, even though no body is present.

18

PLANNING YOUR FUNERAL

As difficult as it is for most people in Canada to face death, planning your funeral, either formally or informally, is part of estate planning. I suppose that if you are still putting off writing your will, you probably are not ready to consider your funeral.

Funerals, like marriages or bar mitzvahs, are a rite of passage, a way to recognize a significant stage of life. The successful Disney movie, "The Lion King" had an award-winning song called "The Circle of Life." More people are now thinking about death as a part of life, as part of an on-going cycle. As we face the aging of the Canadian population, death will become a more frequent occurrence and should be viewed as part of a natural progression.

Nevertheless, death is never an easy topic, and people are often reluctant to consider the funeral decisions that need to be made, either by them or by family on their behalf.

Think of how much time and effort goes into planning another rite of passage, a wedding. Some traditional funerals are as elaborate as the most formal wedding, and yet there may be only a few days to prepare—days when your family is most vulnerable, both emotionally and financially.

Some people feel that significant amounts of money are required to pay tribute to the deceased. There is no one way to celebrate a life. It can be done simply or elaborately. I believe a life is not enhanced or diminished by the amount of money spent on a funeral. Some elaborate, expensive funerals have been arranged by people who later realized that the money did not appease the guilt, or mixed feelings, or stress, or grief they were feeling at the time. There are few "rules" regarding what funeral arrangements are necessary.

EXECUTOR'S RESPONSIBILITY

The final responsibility for arranging your funeral lies with your executor. You can leave specific instructions or provide general guidance regarding your wishes to assist your family and executor. Your executor may legally override your oral or written instructions when they are not appropriate. For example, if you prearrange, but not prepay, an elaborate funeral that the estate cannot afford, your wishes are not likely to be carried out. On the other hand, if you wish a very simple funeral, your instructions may provide the needed guidance to your executor and family, who might otherwise find it difficult to keep from over-spending on the funeral.

Some people put their funeral instructions in their will. Unfortunately, if the will is not found until after your funeral, it will have been impossible to follow those instructions unless you told your family and executor of any special requests you had regarding funeral arrangements, cremation, or organ donation. You might write your instructions down and leave them with your executor, or preplan your funeral (see the "Preplanning" section later in this chapter).

COSTS

Funerals are big business and can be expensive. Costs range from around $1,000 to more than $12,000, depending on the arrangements and the pricing policies of the funeral home, memorial society, or non-profit organization. At one funeral home, the most expensive casket was more than $12,000. But that home also had a casket that cost around $200 and many in between. The most basic funeral is called a transfer service or immediate disposition service, and involves the transfer of the deceased's body from the place of death to the cemetery or crematorium. It may be arranged for around $800.

Discuss your options with a funeral director or counsellor when deciding what you want. You may have strong wishes regarding the type of funeral and the music that you want. One of the ways to plan your funeral is to note of what you like and dislike at the funerals of friends and relatives. There may be a special piece of music, or part of the ceremony that you find particularly appropriate. There may also be a part of the ritual that you do not wish recreated at your funeral.

You may want to arrange other details, such as the newspaper notice, who will be invited, the flowers, and the reception after the service. While some people may find this macabre, others find great comfort in making their own arrangements. You might just want to say to your family that you would like them to do what they think is best, or indicate that you don't want anything fancy.

 Look for somewhere that gives you value for the dollar and has a sensitive funeral director. There should be no pressure from anyone you speak to. If you live in a small community, you may not have many options to choose from, but by preplanning, you can reduce unnecessary pressures and costs to your family.

PREPLANNING

Funeral homes suggest that we should be planning our funerals far in advance. Preplanning is determining your wishes for a funeral in advance of death. It *does not* require any payment in advance or any other financial obligation, but it can help you anticipate the costs and provide information for your executor regarding your wishes.

Through preplanning services, a funeral home can attract and anticipate future business. As a financial advisor, I recognize the importance of planning when making a major consumer purchase—which is what a funeral is. When time is not a factor, you may consider your options and compare the costs of the services and supplies. Use your judgement and select the type of funeral you would like, as well as the type of burial or cremation, as governed by your own wishes, your budget, and the traditions of your community.

Q. *How do I preplan a funeral?*

A. Visit or phone one or more funeral homes. You may pick up their information and price lists or request them by mail. Most funeral homes prefer that you make an appointment to come in and see them to discuss your funeral and are prepared to answer your questions without obligation or any sales pressure.

In some provinces, the arrangements for the funeral and the arrangements for burial, cremation, or interment can be made through the same place. In Ontario, funeral homes and cemeteries are required by law to operate separately, although many have associations with the other.

When planning your funeral, the major decisions include

• burial or cremation?

• if a casket, open or closed, bought or rented?

• embalming?

• service or no service?

• if a service, in a church or chapel?

Refer to the "Funeral Planning Considerations" checklist at the end of this chapter.

Preplanning is on the rise. One funeral home in Toronto told me that it is now preplanning an average of two funerals a day. The ageing demographics of the Canadian population, increased awareness through articles and advertising, different cultural traditions, and concern about controlling funeral costs are all contributing to this trend. Many nursing homes now require that a funeral be prepaid or preplanned before a resident moves in, or that they at least have the name of a funeral director to contact when necessary.

The funeral home will keep personal information such as your date of birth and social insurance number so it can help your family or executor complete the necessary paperwork at the time of death.

PREPAID FUNERALS

Prepaying, or prearranging, a funeral is similar to preplanning, except that the arrangements are planned with a contract and paid for in advance. With the exception of Newfoundland, every province has legislation dealing with prepaid funerals. The funds paid are held "in trust" for you, either by the funeral home or a provincial organization. If you've prepaid your funeral, be sure that your executor knows, so that another funeral is not also arranged and paid for!

Watch out for contracts that simply state that the funds held in trust by the funeral home will go only towards the actual cost of the funeral (with an unwritten implication that the family or the estate will pay any additional amount owing at the time of the funeral). Prepaid funeral contracts should have a clause that states how the funeral will be paid for at the time of death if the amount of the funeral arrangements are more than stated in the contract. Many contracts now state that if, at the time of the funeral, the cost of the details that were prepaid is greater than the amount paid, the funeral home will be responsible for paying the difference. Likewise, the contract should include a clause that states how funds will be returned to the estate if the funeral costs less at the time of death or if the funeral is not handled through that home.

For example, you prepay $4,400 for the funeral services selected. Your contract guarantees that the prearranged services will be fully paid for. The funds earn the current interest rate each year and at the time of death, the amount in trust is $5,390. If the actual cost for the funeral in three years is $5,000, the estate will receive a refund of $390. But if the cost for that funeral is $5,900, the difference should be covered by the funeral home. Your family does not have to write an additional cheque (except for any additional services that they want to include that were not prearranged under the contract).

If you prepay a contract with a purchase price of less than $15,000 (which is much more than the cost of the average funeral), the interest on the funds grows tax-free, unless it is not used for the prepaid services.

As with any contract, determine how flexible the funeral or cemetery contract is.

- What happens if you move?

- Can you obtain a full refund?

- What does the contract say about cancelling it if you change your mind?

- Can you cancel it within 10 or 30 days of signing and obtain a full refund? Or at any time? For example, in British Columbia, a pre-paid plan can be cancelled at any time, but 20% of the amount paid can be withheld. In Ontario, the funeral home may deduct up to 10% of the prepaid funds, to a maximum of $200.

Q. I've purchased a double burial plot. The resale value is now about $10,000. I want to take an extensive trip and be cremated. Can I sell my plot?

A. Refer to the contract that you signed. It should say how cancellation of the contract is to be handled and specify any fees to be withheld.

In some provinces, funeral homes operate separately from cemeteries and crematoriums. If you decide that you wish to buy a burial plot, you might have to arrange this separately.

Besides prepaying the funeral, some of the common ways to pay a funeral bill are to arrange

- a joint bank account with someone who will be responsible for paying for the funeral and burial costs from that account

- for your executor to pay for the funeral from your bank account, if the bank approves the request to provide the funds

- for a family member to pay the expenses and for the estate to reimburse them, or
- to pay for the funeral out of a small insurance policy.

T I P Break-ins have occurred while family members attended a funeral. It would be prudent to have someone house-sit during the funeral.

FUNERAL PLANNING CONSIDERATIONS✓

I would like a

❑ funeral service   ❑ memorial service   ❑ doesn't matter

I would like

the following music to be played: _____

I would like

the following to be read: _____

I would like

❑ flowers

❑ instead of flowers, donations to be made to _____

I prefer to be

❑ buried   ❑ cremated   ❑ doesn't matter

❑ I do   ❑ do not   want an open casket

If cremated, I wish my remains to be:

❑ buried at _____   ❑ scattered at _____

❑ other _____

❑ I have   ❑ have not

preplanned my funeral at _____

❑ I have   ❑ have not

prepaid my funeral at _____

Other special instructions:

_____

_____

_____

_____

19 YOU CAN'T TAKE IT WITH YOU

Depending on your situation and your objectives, estate planning can be fairly straightforward or very complicated. But it is part of the complete financial planning process that evolves as your life does. Your estate plan will affect those people closest to you, your community, and the assets and property that you have saved and managed.

Your estate plan should reflect what is important to *you* and how you would like to distribute your assets. It should meet your needs while you are alive and consider the tax issues, legal issues, and family matters. It can help to ensure there is enough money to pay the taxes and, if your family was dependent on you as a breadwinner, to replace your income. It includes preparing the powerful legal documents. Doing nothing is *not* a responsible option! It is not in the best interests of your family, business, or other relationships.

As I mentioned in the preface, thirty years ago estate planning was fairly simple—the laws and personal finances were relatively straightforward. But today, I beleive that estate planning has a greater impact on everyday Canadians than ever before and that we need to take steps to keep government out of our lives wherever we can. Through estate planning, we can speak for ourselves and our families.

Steps in Developing Your Estate Plan

1) Determine your objectives and goals.

2) Review your personal and business situation and your family dynamics.

3) Review your pre-estate and estate documents.

4) Assess your estate planning issues.

5) Determine the appropriate estate planning strategies.

6) Discuss your plan with those affected, such as your executor and guardians.

7) Implement those strategies.

8) Prepare or update your pre-estate and estate documents.

That said, you do not want to unnecessarily complicate your estate. The roots of your estate plan are your own personal objectives. Whom do *you* want to benefit from your estate: yourself, your beneficiaries, or Revenue Canada? Are you creating a major legacy and leaving as much as possible to your beneficiaries? Or leaving only what is left over after you have enjoyed it? Or is your primary purpose to keep as much as possible from Revenue Canada? This book has discussed some of your options for meeting your objectives.

By planning, you will be able to benefit your beneficiaries the way you envision.

TAX PLANNING

Throughout the book, I have assumed that you do not want Revenue Canada to "benefit" from your estate any more than absolutely necessary. You may also have strong feelings with regard to the size of Revenue Canada's share of your estate.

Estate planning can reduce the taxes and fees that your estate will be required to pay on your death, and result in a smoother transition to your beneficiaries, with less family conflict. Making informed decisions will help you to determine the most effective ways to manage your financial affairs—and ensure that you do not send Revenue Canada any more than necessary, or sooner than necessary.

Because you can transfer assets tax-free to your spouse on death, it makes sense to consider which, if not all, assets to leave to your spouse. And if you have survived your spouse, then you should review your own plan with an eye to making sure that as much as possible goes to the next generation—and not the government. There are tax considerations when assets are left to a spouse (same-generation planning) and other considerations when assets are left to children or grandchildren (inter-generation planning) or charity.

Taxes are never simple, and no matter how well you structure your estate plan, it is likely that governments will collect some tax and will try to get more in the future. Recent tax changes, including the elimination of the personal capital gains exemption, increases in provincial probate fees, and the increased taxation of trusts are just three examples of the direction governments are heading.

WORKING WITH PROFESSIONALS

I believe that there is no substitute for professional advice. But many people find it challenging to find and work with competent professionals they feel they can trust. Professionals can give you advice tailored to your particular situation (which a book *cannot* do), direct you on the most efficient course of action, and ensure that you have taken care of all of the details. You might be working with a team of professionals who are all experts in their particular area. The team might include a trust officer, financial advisor, life insurance representative, a lawyer specializing in family, corporate, or estate law, and an accountant, to name just a few.

One of the best ways to locate a good professional is by word of mouth. Remember, finding a good advisor is a lot like finding a good family doctor: it takes competency and the right chemistry mix as well. You should feel comfortable with the individual and feel they care about you. If you are not comfortable with them, you may not take their advice, or you may take their advice without questioning it, and neither is good for your financial health. None of your advisors should intimidate you.

Take advantage of the free initial consultation offered by many professionals (although there is a trend to charge for this meeting if advice is given). Be prepared to discuss your situation, your concerns, your values, and your goals. If you are used to being very private about your financial affairs, you may at first feel a bit awkward discussing your family and financial situation. This initial meeting will help you to determine whether you feel comfortable with the advisor on a personal level, as well as give you an opportunity to assess their competency.

The advisor should look comprehensively at your financial health, understand your needs, answer your questions, and ensure confidentiality in your relationship. Look for experience, credentials, high ethical standards, community involvement, and dedication to their clients. While not all advisors currently consider their clients' estate planning needs, I expect this will be a growing area of specialization as the population of Canada ages.

Sometimes, your advisors may ask you questions that make you question your own decisions. For example, if you are naming your eldest daughter as your power of attorney, the lawyer might ask whether you are sure you can trust her. Their questions are designed to help protect your interests. Think through your decisions a second time, but don't stop relying on your own judgement if it has served you well over the years.

IT'S AN ONGOING PROCESS

Estate planning is an ongoing (but not frequent) process. Tax laws and family and succession laws continually change, as do the market values of property and other assets. Family members come and go. If you are raising a family and have not yet accumulated significant savings, your primary concern may be to create an estate for your dependants through life insurance. As both your savings and children grow, you may be more concerned with providing a tax-effective transfer of assets. Your estate plan will need to be updated to reflect these changes.

For example, my will was first written in 1980, after our first son was born. If I had not taken the time to update it, I would not have addressed these important changes:

• additional children

• changes to Ontario family law

• the increased size of our assets

• the increased sophistication in the types of investments in my portfolio

• the use of spousal trusts

• changes to the personal circumstances of our named guardian and her ability to act in that capacity.

As taxes increase and legislation becomes more powerful, it is important to ask the correct questions to achieve financial success. Tax and investment decisions also have implications for your estate, and estate planning strategies are key to a successful financial plan—but are often overlooked! One of my objectives in writing this book was to help you ask the correct questions so that you, with your advisors, can determine and implement strategies that are appropriate for your situation.

NOW DO IT!

It is not a matter of "if" you should do estate planning. The integration of today's needs, retirement and tax planning, and investment management will help ensure your financial security and peace of mind. None of these aspects can be adequately dealt with without considering the others. Estate planning is just part of financial planning.

It may take some time to implement your estate plan. You may choose to discuss your estate plans with your family to ensure that you organize your affairs in the best way possible for all concerned. For example, you may have trouble deciding which of your three children should inherit the cottage, when in reality none of them wants it at all. Your family may be genuinely concerned for your future, and in fact they may even experience a sense of relief knowing that you have thoroughly considered your options and documented your wishes. In other families, relatives may just want to know how much they will be getting.

Estate planning is not easy, because it makes us face the fact that we are mortal. As you plan your estate, you may struggle with what you have or have not accumulated during your lifetime, with your family relationships, with making the "right" decisions. You may even be dealing with professionals for the very first time. I hope that by now you feel a little more comfortable and ready to discuss how some of the strategies may fit your personal situation.

When your estate plan is in place, you may experience a sense that everything is in order, and that your financial affairs are organized in an effective, efficient manner to meet your own needs and to benefit future generations. Along with a feeling that you have done the right thing, you may even have a sense of relief. If you can sleep at night with your decisions and have reviewed them with your professional advisors, then you've taken positive steps.

Self-assessment is an important phase in financial planning. I hope you will take the time to complete the "Personal Inventory" at the end of this book to review where you are today.

My hope is that the information in this book, and your "homework," will save you money today and pay big benefits, financial and otherwise, to your beneficiaries. Their future depends on it.

After all, you can't take it with you!

20
GETTING ORGANIZED AND KEEPING RECORDS

"My husband was what you might call 'old school.' When he died, I didn't know anything about our financial situation. I thought I was destitute. Eventually, we located a will, bonds, insurance policies ... lots of money. I guess that I should have been relieved, but I was angry. Angry at myself for not knowing, and angry at him for not letting me know."

C.

Part of estate planning is getting organized. The information in this chapter brings together everything that came before in this book. Now it's time to get organized.

When someone dies, all their important documents need to be found—the will, birth certificate, life insurance policies, company benefits information, safety deposit box and key, bank accounts, pension plans, RRSP and RRIF accounts, ownership papers for specific assets and property, and other important papers. You can assist your executor and spouse (and make it easier for your family) by organizing your financial papers and writing down where they will find your will and your personal details. The more account numbers, addresses, contact names, and other information you provide, the more you help your executor do their job. And if your power of attorney needs to step in before your death, being organized will also help him or her.

Not a problem, you say. But Canadians have enough trouble locating their own papers to complete their income tax each year! One family was trying to settle the father's affairs after he died. He had been very secretive all his life about his money. Not knowing where to find even a list of all his accounts and property dragged out the settling of his estate. Just when they thought that it was all settled, something new was uncovered.

SIMPLIFY, SIMPLIFY, SIMPLIFY

While you are getting organized, it may be useful to remove some of the complexity from your financial matters. One step in estate planning is to take a look at your overall financial affairs and to consider how complex those affairs are. Do you really need four RRSPs, five bank accounts, and three brokerage accounts? What may make life simpler for your estate might also make your own life simpler and easier to manage, if you don't give up any investor protection. Just as one example, you might deposit your stocks in an account with a brokerage firm, rather than leaving them in a safety deposit box. The monthly statement would provide a handy inventory of your investments.

Q. My spouse and I have signing authority for our safety deposit box and my daughter knows the location of the key in case something happens to us. Is there anything else we should do?

A. Yes. The key alone is not enough. Your daughter has no authority to go into your safety deposit box unless she has signing access. To give her authority (if this is what you want to do), have her name and signature added to the safety deposit box signature card.

I've included a Personal Inventory form and questionnaires on the pages that follow to help you

- assess your current financial situation

- determine your estate planning objectives

- identify questions for your lawyer, financial advisor, accountant, or other professional

- instruct your advisors

- make it easier for your executor to locate all your documents.

Don't try to complete all the information in one sitting. Give yourself time to think through your situation and what would be best for your circumstances. Once the forms are completed, keeping the information up to date will not take nearly as long. Annual updating seems to work for most people, such as around tax time or near the end of the year.

To receive a copy of these forms, or my estate planning seminar on tape, complete the order form at the back of the book.

Someday you've got to get organized. Keeping good records is one of the cheapest (if not the simplest) estate planning strategies to implement.

PERSONAL INVENTORY

Basic Information

Date prepared: _____

Date updated: _____

Date updated: _____

Name _____

Full legal name (if different) _____

Date of birth _____ Place of birth _____

Occupation _____

Employer _____ Employee number _____

Home phone _____ Business phone _____

Home address _____ Business name _____

Business address _____

_____

Fax number _____

DESCRIPTION OF RELATIVES

SPOUSE ❏ YES   ❏ NO

Name _____

Date of marriage _____

Location of marriage certificate _____

Marriage contract ❏ YES   ❏ NO   Location _____

COMMON-LAW SPOUSE   ❏ YES   ❏ NO

Name _____

Date of co-habitation _____

Living together contract   ❏ YES   ❏ NO

Location _____

SEPARATED?   ❏ YES   ❏ NO

If yes, date of separation _____

Separation agreement   ❏ YES   ❏ NO

Location _____

Address of spouse _____

DIVORCED? ❏ YES   ❏ NO

If yes, date of divorce (absolute received) _____

Location of divorce agreement _____

Name of ex-spouse _____

Address of ex-spouse _____

Do support obligations continue for ex-spouse after your death?   ❏ YES   ❏ NO

WIDOWED?   ❏ YES   ❏ NO

If yes, date of spouse's death _____

Photocopy page if more space is required.

CHILDREN OF PRESENT MARRIAGE ❑ YES ❑ NO

Name _____ Date of birth_____
Address _____
Marital status _____ Disabled ❑ YES ❑ NO
If married, name of child's spouse _____

Name _____ Date of birth_____
Address _____
Marital status _____ Disabled ❑ YES ❑ NO
If married, name of spouse _____

Name _____ Date of birth_____
Address _____
Marital status _____ Disabled ❑ YES ❑ NO
If married, name of child's spouse _____

Name _____ Date of birth_____
Address _____
Marital status _____ Disabled ❑ YES ❑ NO
If married, name of spouse _____

CHILDREN OF PREVIOUS MARRIAGE ❑ YES ❑ NO

Name _____ Date of birth_____
Address _____
Marital status _____ Disabled ❑ YES ❑ NO
If married, name of child's spouse _____

Name _____ Date of birth_____
Address _____
Marital status _____ Disabled ❑ YES ❑ NO
If married, name of child's spouse _____

Do maintenance and support obligations continue after death? ❑ YES ❑ NO

Photocopy page if more space is required.

OTHER CHILDREN

Name _____ Date of birth_____

Address _____

Marital status _____

Name of other parent _____

Name _____ Date of birth_____

Address _____

Marital status _____

Name of other parent _____

GRANDCHILDREN

Name _____ Date of birth_____

Address _____

Name of parents _____

Name _____ Date of birth_____

Address _____

Name of parents _____

Name _____ Date of birth_____

Address _____

Name of parents _____

Name _____ Date of birth_____

Address _____

Name of parents _____

Name _____ Date of birth_____

Address _____

Name of parents _____

Photocopy page if more space is required.

DOCUMENTS FOR YOUR ESTATE PLAN

Location of birth certificate _____

Location of citizenship papers _____

Social Insurance Number _____

    Location of SIN card _____

Will prepared?   ❏ YES   ❏ NO

    Location of original will _____

    Location of copy of will _____

    Date last reviewed _____

Power of attorney for financial decisions prepared?   ❏ YES   ❏ NO

    Location of power of attorney for financial decisions

    _____

    Date last reviewed _____

Is there a separate power of attorney in effect at the bank? ❏ YES ❏ NO

Power of attorney for personal care proxy prepared?   ❏ YES   ❏ NO

    Location of power of attorney for personal care

    _____

    Date last reviewed _____

Living will prepared?   ❏ YES   ❏ NO

    Location of living will _____

    Date last reviewed _____

Organ/tissue donation form completed?   ❏ YES   ❏ NO

    Location of signed organ donor form _____

    Date last reviewed _____

Advance medical directive prepared?   ❏ YES   ❏ NO

    Location of advance medical directive _____

    Date last reviewed _____

Trust currently in effect?   ❏ YES   ❏ NO

    Location of trust documents _____

    Name of trustee _____

    Date last reviewed _____

    Are inter vivos trusts to be set up?   ❏ YES   ❏ NO

Are you a war veteran?   ❏ YES   ❏ NO

    Location of discharge papers and service record

    _____

Income tax returns _____

    Year last filed _____

    Location of income tax returns _____

    Location of receipts for current year _____

Have you prearranged a funeral?   ❏ YES   ❏ NO

    Name of funeral company _____

    Address _____

    Location of preplanned agreement _____

    Prepaid funeral?   ❏ YES   ❏ NO

    Contract no. _____

PROFESSIONAL ADVISORS

List those people who provide you with professional advice.

	Name	Phone
Accountant	_____	_____
Bank manager	_____	_____
Family doctor	_____	_____
Other health care professional	_____	_____
Financial advisor	_____	_____
Insurance agent	_____	_____
Lawyer	_____	_____
Minister/priest/ rabbi/other clergy	_____	_____
Relative	_____	_____
Stockbroker	_____	_____
Trust officer	_____	_____
Other	_____	_____

ASSETS*

BANK ACCOUNTS

Name of bank _____

Address _____

Account no. _____

Type of account _____

Registered owners _____

Approx. balance _____

CANADA SAVINGS BONDS

Bond holder account number _____

Series and registration numbers _____

Registered owners _____

Location _____ Amount_____

GICS, CERTIFICATE OF DEPOSITS, TERM DEPOSITS
(attach latest statements)

Institution _____

Address _____

Certificate number _____

Value _____ Maturity date _____

Registered owners _____

RRSPS/GRRSPS/RRIFS/LIFS/DPSPS
(attach latest statements)

Institution _____

Address _____

Account number/type _____

Beneficiary _____

Market value _____

* *If you held these assets prior to marriage, also indicate the value at the date of marriage.*

Photocopy page if more space is required.

SAFETY DEPOSIT BOX

Institution _____

Address _____

Box no. _____ Who has signing authority? _____

Location of key to safety deposit box _____

Contents of safety deposit box (attach a list) _____

STOCKS *(attach latest statements)*

Registered owners _____

Company and address _____

Market value _____

Adjusted cost/V-day value*_____

MUTUAL FUNDS *(attach latest statements)*

Registered owners _____

Company and address _____

Market value _____

Adjusted cost/V-day value*_____

BONDS/DEBENTURES

Registered owners _____

Company and address _____

Market value _____

Adjusted cost/V-day value*_____

TAX SHELTER INVESTMENTS
*(oil and gas, mutual fund, limited partnerships,
real estate partnerships, films, etc.)*

Registered owners _____

Company and address _____

Market value _____

Adjusted cost/V-day value*_____

Photocopy page if more space is required.

PRIVATE LOANS/MORTGAGES HELD *(include promissory notes)*

Name and address of debtor _____

_____

Outstanding balance _____

Terms of loan _____

Is this loan/mortgage to be forgiven on your death? ❑ YES ❑ NO

GOLD/SILVER

Type _____

Location _____

OTHER INVESTMENTS

_____

_____

LIFE INSURANCE POLICIES *(Group and Individual)*

Company and address _____

Policy number _____

Type of policy _____

Death benefit _____

Beneficiary _____

Cash value _____

Outstanding policy loan? ❑ YES   ❑ NO

ANNUITIES *(include Gift Annuities)*

Company and address _____

Contract number _____

Annual income _____

Monthly payment _____

Guaranteed period _____

Beneficiary _____

Photocopy page if more space is required.

PENSION PLANS *(include former employers where applicable)*

    Company and address _____

    Reference no. _____

    Amount and type of survivor benefit _____

    Beneficiary _____

CARS, VANS, TRUCKS, BOATS

    Model _____

    Year _____

    Ownership _____

    Cost _____

    Market value _____

ANTIQUES, ARTWORK, JEWELLERY, SPECIAL COLLECTIONS
(valued over $1,000)

    Description of item _____

    Location _____

    Owner _____

    Cost _____

    Appraised value _____

REAL ESTATE
(Principal Residence)

    Address _____

    Registered owners _____

    Amount of mortgage _____

    Amount of reverse mortgage _____

    Date purchased _____

    Cost _____

    Market value _____

    Location of deed _____

Photocopy page if more space is required.

VACATION PROPERTIES
(cottage, condo, timeshare, etc.)

   Address _____

   Registered owners _____

   Amount of mortgage _____

   Date purchased _____

   Cost _____

   Market value _____

   Location of deed _____

INVESTMENT PROPERTIES

   Address _____

   Registered owners _____

   Amount of mortgage _____

   Date purchased _____

   Cost _____

   Market value _____

   Location of deed _____

If the property has tenants

   Names of tenants _____

   Date lease renews _____

ASSETS/PROPERTY OUTSIDE CANADA

   Country _____

   Description of asset _____

   Registered owners _____

   Date purchased _____

   Cost _____

   Market value _____

Photocopy page if more space is required.

BUSINESS

Ownership of business _____

Business name _____

Address _____

Nature of business _____

Fair market value _____

Proprietorship ❑ YES ❑ NO

Location of business records _____

Location of unpaid invoices _____

Partnership ❑ YES ❑ NO
If a partnership,

Name of partners _____

Nature of the partnership agreement _____

Location of partnership agreement _____

Is there a buy-sell agreement? ❑ YES ❑ NO

If yes, how will a buyout be funded? _____

Corporation ❑ YES ❑ NO
If a corporation,

Name of major shareholders _____

Any restrictions on the transfer of shares? ❑ YES ❑ NO

Is there a shareholders' or buy-sell agreement? ❑ YES ❑ NO

If yes, how will a buyout be funded? _____

OTHER ASSETS

_____

_____

_____

Are any assets the result of a gift or an inheritance? ❑ YES ❑ NO

If yes, indicate those that are _____

_____

Do you have an interest in an estate or trust that provides a bene-fit to your estate? ❑ YES ❑ NO

If yes,

Name of estate trust _____

Value of trust interest _____

LIABILITIES AND DEBTS

Credit Cards

    Institution and address _____

    Card number _____

    Balance owing _____

    Balance insured? _____

Lines of Credit

    Institution and address _____

    Account number _____

    Balance owing _____

    Balance insured? _____

Loans / Promissory Notes / Guarantees

    Institution and address _____

    Loan number _____

    Balance owing _____

    Balance insured? _____

Mortgages Payable by You

    Institution and address _____

    Mortgage number _____

    Balance owing _____

    Balance insured? _____

Reverse Mortgage

    Institution and address _____

    Mortgage number _____

    Balance owing _____

    Balance insured? _____

Photocopy page if more space is required.

Other Liabilities

    Description _____ Amount _____

    Description _____ Amount _____

    Description _____ Amount _____

    Description _____ Amount _____

CONSIDERATIONS WHEN WRITING YOUR WILL*

BEQUESTS

How do you want your estate distributed?
Entire estate to spouse? ❑ YES ❑ NO

If not all to spouse:

_____

_____

_____

_____

_____

Do you need a marriage contract to ensure that the instructions in your will can be carried out? ❑ YES ❑ NO

Are there specific items, family heirlooms, or sums of money you want to go to specific individuals or charities?

What	To whom	*(circle one)*
_____ Spouse _____		
_____ Children _____		per stirpes / per capita
_____ Grandchildren _____		per stirpes / per capita
_____ Others _____		

Residue to be distributed as follows to

All to spouse? ❑ YES ❑ NO

If not all to spouse:

What	To whom	*(circle one)*
_____ Spouse _____		
_____ Children _____		per stirpes / per capita
_____ Grandchildren _____		per stirpes / per capita
_____ Others _____		

*These pages are **not** a will.*

Have you provided for your spouse according to the family law or matrimonial property law in your province?

_____

_____

Is the bequest or residue to be left outright, or to be held in trust?

_____

Is the distribution of your estate tax effective?

_____

Are you holding loans or mortgages for family members that you want forgiven at your death?

_____

Who will prepare your will?

_____

EXECUTOR

Does your executor know the location of your will?

_____

Is your spouse to be your executor?   ❑ YES   ❑ NO

If not your spouse, who would you like to be your executor(s)?

Name _____   Name _____

Address _____   Address _____

*These pages are **not** a will.*

Do you want your executor to have the power to postpone the sale of assets, to select the investments, to make elections under the *Income Tax Act*, transfer assets in kind to beneficiaries rather than to liquidate assets and pay cash to beneficiaries?
❑ YES   ❑ NO

Do you want to give your executor the authorization to purchase any assets of the estate?
❑ YES   ❑ NO

JOINT DISASTER

In the event you and your spouse are killed in a common disaster:

How is your estate to be distributed?

_____

_____

Are your children underage?   ❑ YES   ❑ NO

TESTAMENTARY TRUSTS FOR MINOR BENEFICIARIES

Is a testamentary trust to be set up for:
Spouse   ❑ YES   ❑ NO
Children/grandchildren   ❑ YES   ❑ NO
Disabled beneficiary   ❑ YES   ❑ NO
Name of the proposed trustee _____

Have you discussed your wishes with your trustee?
❑ YES   ❑ NO

Is capital to be distributed to children/grandchildren at the age of 18?
❑ YES   ❑ NO

If no, then at what age(s)? _____

Should your trustee have the power to encroach on income and/or capital for the benefit of the beneficiaries?
❏ YES ❏ NO
Do you have specific wishes as to how the income and capital are to be used?
❏ YES ❏ NO
Instructions for trustee _____

Investment Powers of the Trust

Limited powers ❏ YES ❏ NO
Discretionary powers ❏ YES ❏ NO

GUARDIANS

If children are under 18, proposed guardian
Name _____
Address _____
Relationship to you _____

Alternate guardian(s) for children

Name _____
Address _____
Relationship to you _____
Have you discussed your wishes with these people?
❏ YES ❏ NO

DEPENDANTS

Names of any people, in addition to your spouse and children, who are financially dependent on you:
(grandchild / brother / sister / parent / same-sex partner / common-law spouse/etc.)

Name	Relationship	Amount of support annually
_____	_____	_____
_____	_____	_____
_____	_____	_____

Ontario: Do you wish to include wording to protect any inheritance passed to your children/grandchildren in the event of their divorce?   ❑ YES   ❑ NO

CONSIDERATIONS WHEN REVIEWING YOUR WILL

Every few years, review your will to ensure it continues to meet your needs. Events that occur in your life could directly affect your estate plan. Your will needs to accurately reflect your wishes and your situation at the time of your death.

If you answer "yes" or "unsure" to any of the following questions, get your will updated. If the changes are not extensive, your will can be updated using a codicil. If the changes are extensive, your instructions may be clearer if you prepare a new will.

If it took you years to get around to preparing your first will, don't take as long to get around to reviewing it!

Since your will was prepared, have you

	Yes	No	Unsure
Married? Divorced? Been widowed?	❑	❑	❑
Signed a marriage contract?	❑	❑	❑
Separated?	❑	❑	❑
Had or adopted a child?	❑	❑	❑
Lost (death) a child? or grandchild?	❑	❑	❑
Gained grandchildren?	❑	❑	❑
Added dependants: ageing parents, children returned home?	❑	❑	❑
Loaned money to your children?	❑	❑	❑
Increased/decreased your net worth significantly?	❑	❑	❑
Acquired new property, such as a cottage?	❑	❑	❑
Received an inheritance or significant gift?	❑	❑	❑
Made a substantial gift?	❑	❑	❑
Started a business?	❑	❑	❑
Purchased life insurance?	❑	❑	❑
Started a retirement plan? RRSP? pension?	❑	❑	❑
Moved to a new province or country?	❑	❑	❑
Decided to add/remove a beneficiary?	❑	❑	❑

	Yes	No	Unsure
Started to receive income from a trust?	❏	❏	❏
Thought about making a planned gift?	❏	❏	❏

In addition:

	Yes	No	Unsure
Have any of your children turned 18?	❏	❏	❏
Have any of your children married? remarried? separated?	❏	❏	❏
Have any changes occurred to the *Income Tax Act?*	❏	❏	❏
Have there been any changes to family law in your province?	❏	❏	❏
Have any of your beneficiaries predeceased you?	❏	❏	❏
Has your executor or guardian moved?	❏	❏	❏
Is your executor now unwilling or unable to perform the duties of executor?	❏	❏	❏
Does it look like you will outlive your executor?	❏	❏	❏
Is the person named as guardian now unwilling or unable to perform the duties of guardian?	❏	❏	❏
Are the liabilities your estate will face on your death greater than the value of your liquid assets?	❏	❏	❏
Should you set up an inter vivos trust outside your will?	❏	❏	❏

ASSETS AND LIABILITIES AT DEATH (1)

Calculating the liabilities and taxes due on death is not an exact science. The worksheets will give you a rough estimate. These amounts must be reviewed periodically to reflect current market values and tax rules.

I have included two worksheets to estimate your assets and liabilities at death: one for same-generation estate planning, for an individual who expects to be survived by a spouse or common-law spouse, and one where the assets will be passing from one generation to the next. If you have a spouse, I recommend that you complete both worksheets and use the second worksheet assuming that your spouse dies before you.

ASSETS PASSING TO YOUR SPOUSE

What will your estate be dealing with if it is being passed to your spouse?

LIQUID ASSETS

These are the assets that could be turned into cash quickly and relatively easily. Do not include any assets that are registered jointly with rights of survivorship with someone other than your spouse.

Cash in bank accounts	_____
Canada Savings Bonds	_____
Treasury Bills	_____
Cashable term deposits or GICs	_____
RRSPs*	_____
RRIFs*	_____
LIFs*	_____
DPSPs*	_____
Life insurance paid to "Estate"	_____
CPP lump-sum death benefit	_____
Lump-sum company pension benefits	_____

Total liquid assets   _____

* If you have named a beneficiary other than your spouse, enter NIL.

NON-LIQUID ASSETS

These are the assets that may take longer to turn into cash, or that you may want to leave intact for the benefit of your beneficiaries. Do not include any assets that are registered jointly with rights of survivorship with someone other than your spouse.

Principal residence   _____

Business   _____

Investment property   _____

Vacation property   _____

Assets not maturing in the next
12 months   _____

Vehicles   _____

Personal items   _____

Other   _____

Total non-liquid assets   _____

LIABILITIES

These are some of the expenses that your estate will need to settle on your death. If your total liabilities are greater than your total liquid assets, your executor may need to sell some of your non-liquid assets to pay off the bills.

Estimated Income Tax on

Income in the year of death   _____

Capital gains * **   _____

Collapsing RRSPs or RRIFs*   _____

Previous year's income tax return _____

Recapture of capital cost
allowance and terminal loss   _____

Less capital losses/prepaid
taxes   _____

Estimated income tax   _____

U.S. estate tax   _____

Funeral expenses (if not prepaid)   _____

Liabilities related to a business   _____

Probate fees   _____

Legal fees   _____

Continuing support payments   _____

Trustee fees   _____

Outstanding loans and/or mortgages   _____

Outstanding balance of reverse mortgage_____

Credit card balances   _____

Other liabilities   _____

Total liabilities (estimated)   _____

Do you have enough liquid assets to pay off the liabilities?
❑ YES   ❑ NO

> * *If you expect to transfer these assets to a surviving spouse or common-law spouse, enter NIL.*
> ***Increases in the value prior to 1972 are tax-free (capital gains started in 1972).*

ASSETS AND LIABILITIES AT DEATH (2)

ASSETS PASSING WHERE THERE IS NO SPOUSE

What will your estate be dealing with if you are not survived by your spouse or common-law spouse (where your estate is passed to the next generation)?

LIQUID ASSETS

These are the assets that could be turned into cash quickly and easily. Do not include any assets that are registered jointly with rights of survivorship.

Cash in bank accounts	_____
Canada Savings Bonds	_____
Treasury Bills	_____
Cashable term deposits or GICs	_____
RRSPs*	_____
RRIFs*	_____
LIFs*	_____
DPSPs*	_____
Life insurance paid to "Estate"	_____
CPP lump-sum death benefit	_____
Lump-sum company pension benefits	_____
Total liquid assets	_____

If you have named a beneficiary, enter NIL.

NON-LIQUID ASSETS

These are the assets that may take longer to turn into cash, or that you may want to leave intact for the benefit of your beneficiaries. Do not include any assets that are registered jointly with rights of survivorship.

Principal residence	_____
Business	_____
Investment property	_____
Vacation property	_____
Assets not maturing in the next 12 months	_____
Vehicles	_____
Personal items	_____
Other	_____
Total non-liquid assets	_____

LIABILITIES

These are some of the expenses that your estate will need to settle on your death. If your total liabilities are greater than your total liquid assets, your executor may need to sell some of your non-liquid assets to pay off the bills.

Estimated income tax on

Income in the year of death	_____
Capital gains**	_____
Collapsing RRSPs or RRIFs	_____
Previous year's income tax return	_____
Recapture of capital cost allowance and terminal loss	_____
Less capital losses/prepaid taxes	_____
Estimated Income tax	_____

U.S. estate tax	_____
Funeral expenses (if not prepaid)	_____
Liabilities related to a business	_____
Probate fees	_____
Legal fees	_____
Continuing support payments	_____
Trustee fees	_____
Outstanding loans and/or mortgages	_____
Outstanding balance of reverse mortgage	_____
Credit card balances	_____
Other liabilities	_____
Total liabilities (estimated)	_____

Do you have enough liquid assets to pay off the liabilities?
❑ YES   ❑ NO

** Increases in the value prior to 1972 are tax-free
(capital gains started in 1972).*

Questions for my lawyer

_____

_____

_____

_____

Questions for my financial advisor

_____

_____

_____

_____

Questions for my insurance agent

_____

_____

_____

_____

Questions for my accountant

_____

_____

_____

_____

Questions for my trust officer

_____

_____

_____

_____

ORDER FORM

To order copies of the "Personal Inventory form" (on 8.5 x 11 paper or on disk) or my estate planning seminar on audio tape, please complete the following information.

Name _____

Address _____

Street _____ Apt/Suite _____

City _____ Province _____

Postal Code _____

Phone Number (____) _____

Fax Number (____) _____

Personal Inventory Forms (on 8.5 x 11 paper)

    Number of sets ordered _____ at $11.99 each = _____

Personal Inventory Forms (on disk)

    Number of sets ordered _____ at $15.99 each = _____
    Specify ❏ Lotus ❏ Excel

Sandra Foster's "Estate Planning" audio tape

    Number of tapes ordered _____ at $19.99 each = _____

                             Total Order = _____

Shipping and handling

(for orders under $30) $5.00   _____

(for orders between $30.01 and $50) $6.00   _____

(for orders over $50) $7.50   _____

                  Subtotal   = _____

                  Provincial Sales Tax   _____

                  G.S.T. 7%   _____

                  Total payment enclosed_____

Mail your order with your cheque or money order made payable to:
CARAT COMMUNICATIONS INC.
4936 Yonge St., Suite 252
North York, Ontario, M2N 6S3

Please allow 4-6 weeks for delivery.

SUGGESTIONS AND SEMINARS

If you have comments, opinions, or are interested in having me conduct seminars or workshops for your group or association, please contact me through one of the methods below.

by fax: (416) 494-9530

through my publisher: John Wiley & Sons Canada, Ltd.
5353 Dundas St. West, 4th Floor
Etobicoke, Ontario, M9B 6H8

by e-mail: fosters@idirect.com

on the internet: http://web.idirect.com/ ~ carat

INDEX